ADVANCE PRAISE

"I loved *The Book of Manifesting* and – rarely for me –
have read it three times over the last few weeks, gaining
more insights each time . . . I've read many books on
manifestation, but none that are as inspirational and
motivational . . . the most original and helpful book on
manifestation I've read."

— *Llewellyn author, Richard Webster*

"*The Book of Manifesting* is about as comprehensive a
spiritual guidebook as I have ever read. In fact it is the
most comprehensive! ...and covers every legitimate
plus practical question a sincere seeker could ever ask."

—*Spirit channel, William Perry*

The Book
of
Manifesting

Spirit—Mind—Body
Flowing—Allowing—Receiving

PAUL GORMAN

Year of the Book
135 Glen Avenue
Glen Rock, PA 17327

ISBN 13: 978-1-64649-389-0 (print)
ISBN 13: 978-1-64649-390-6 (ebook)

Cover photo by author, Western Maryland

Interior images licensed by Depositphotos.com
unless otherwise noted.

Library of Congress Control Number: 2024902989

Disclaimer:
You manifested this book in front of you.
Consider yourself a healed illumination in
the Mind of God.

CONTENTS

"Yet fame or fortune may take wings and fly away, or fortune may become that stumbling stone over which mental and spiritual things are forgotten."

—Edgar Cayce

FOREWORD

This book is about healing the mind. A healed mind can manifest what it wants, but a healed mind doesn't want for anything—so it manifests its desires. It is simple, but not easy. As adults, we are manifesting all the time—what we want, and often what we do not want.

What is a healed mind? —One that allows loving thoughts, and halts non-loving thoughts. A peaceful mind that halts non-loving thoughts illuminates in the light of Oneness—the energy of God Mind.

Imagine a perfectly clean window in your mind with the light coming in. What you see through the window outside are your dreams of goodness that are projected with the light you are receiving.

Would you allow, or even invite others to throw muck onto your clean window? Would it help you to see your dreams? You would not intentionally allow it because the views that you desire—the personal universe you are creating—would be ruined. You may even stop looking out. Others can do what they want, but not on your window. Your window will allow only a clear and unobstructed view to the goodness that you are effortlessly manifesting.

This book thoroughly explores how to create the reality you desire—a manifestation of all that you are *flowing, allowing, and receiving.*

INTRODUCTION

It was not my intention to write a book about manifesting, but in the fall of 2023, I was inspired to do so.

I receive messages from "Oneness," and at that time had been asking questions for myself about manifesting. It occurred to me to explore the topic fully, and then to compile the conversations into a book format so that others could benefit from them.

Now you have acquired this book. I hope you enjoy the information I have received, and I know that you can enhance your life with it. In conversations with Oneness, and in a question and answer format, this book examines how we mentally create our physical realities. I am the scribe, the messenger, and interviewer—trying to understand the answers that I was receiving as I directed the questioning.

What is 'Oneness'? It says, *"I am no thing, meaning the illusion of everything as light... allowing the mind an adventure in life's illusion of twoness."*

Oneness could also be called 'Love' or 'God Mind'. The terminology in this book uses 'God', 'God Mind', and the 'Mind of God' interchangeably, and 'God Mind' is used mostly going forward.

What is 'twoness'? It is the world of separation, perceived by the left side of our brains through our judgments, and often our fears.

Before reading this book, I recommend watching the 18-minute TEDTalk video *My Stroke of Insight* by neuroscientist Dr. Jill Bolte Taylor.[1] She experienced a stroke, and relates what it was like to switch from perceiving reality from the logical and linear left-brain hemisphere, and then to experience it from the abstract and intuitive right-brain hemisphere. It is important to know because throughout this book it is mentioned how our left brain (life-mind) heals into our right brain (Light Mind), and opens in God Mind.

I am not especially religious, but was raised on Catholic stories of mystics and prophets, angels and saints, miracles and healing. Maybe they were just that—stories—but stories to illustrate the truth. I am interested in the truth.

I also had a long career as an architect, and a Frank Lloyd Wright quote comes to mind. He said, "Nature is my church." It is repeated here because 'nature' is discussed several times in the answers to my questions in this book.

How do I receive my information? I ask questions and receive the answers by dowsing—using a pendulum over an alphabet chart. Years ago, a friend had further instructed me by saying, "Ask your higher self. It will

---

[1] http://DrJillTaylor.com

not lie to you." I learned while writing this book that our 'higher self' is God Mind.

My book, *Dowsing Stories: Intuition Speaks,* highlights numerous examples of my dowsing experiences to receive and also to send information using a pendulum—from distance healing with spontaneous remissions, to communicating with birds and insects, making clouds disappear, and even changing the weather—illustrating the interactive nature of our universes.

Will this book help you to win the lottery? Maybe! People win all the time. Winning the lottery could be for your highest good. Sometimes a lesson in detachment is also for our highest good. I hope so—I've had plenty!

Once I did a presentation in a bookstore and demonstrated for an employee there by adjusting his energy frequency to the Frequency of Prosperity. Three weeks later, I was in China and received an email from the bookstore owner saying that the employee had won the lottery—many tens of millions of dollars.

NEWS

WORLD

Lottery winner credits New Age book store

_____ says a New Age book store made it possible for him to become an overnight multimillionaire.

I also later learned that he promptly lost all the money within a year. A message I received at the time said that most people do not win, and others lose after they win. I occasionally play mid-level lottery games, with random, machine-generated numbers. My tickets have 10 plays or more, so it seems that I usually win something—and avoid getting my feelings hurt with a 'Not a Winner' slip!

One year ago, I broke my foot and couldn't walk or drive for three months. The day before, I had said, "I wish I could stop running around."

Recently, my neighbor said that he was sorry it had happened to me. My reply was that I am glad it happened. I learned to work from home more, and was able to spend full-time with our older, deaf Border Collie, Shadow—who declined and passed away—as I got better and was able to help him. I also completed and published *Infinite Healing: Poems and Messages for the Loss of Your Animal Companion* at that time.

These examples illustrate that our words and intentions shape our realities. Having a peaceful mind connects us to God Mind, and healing our minds enables us to create the realities we want.

We are manifesters and are here in the world of *light* and *motion* to heal and to learn—the easy way, or the hard way—in life, or in the moment our physical lives end.

I choose healing in life—the easy way. [Hint: *motion* toward the *light*.]

The God Mind answers to my questions are typically matter-of-fact, sometimes profound, always interesting, often light-hearted, and even comical. 'Light-hearted' is an appropriate term, and is a good description of many of the conversations. Note that the terms 'life-mind' and 'Light Mind' used throughout this book refer to the left-brain hemisphere (life-mind), and the right-brain hemisphere (Light Mind). Simple exercises and affirmations recommended are listed at the end for easy reference. With that preface, enjoy *The Book of Manifesting* as related from God Mind.

Below is a message I received after I had completed writing all of the chapters, shared here as an introduction to God Mind wisdom.

The topic was about atoms having intelligence, and silently communicating with each other.

WHAT WOULD THEY SAY?

What would a tree say to me?
Allow me to create oxygen for you, healing in your blood.

Allow me to absorb carbon dioxide for you, eliminating impurities in your blood.

Allow me to create heating wood for you in my branches, and lumber for you in my trunk.

Allow me to shade you in the heat, and block the winter wind.

I am not able to move more than bending—learn from my flexible nature.

What would a bird say to me?

Allow me to chirp for each new day beginning.

Allow me to eliminate bugs annoying to you, and allow me to sing healing songs to you.

Allow my healing songs to activate God, illuminating in you.

I am able to fly like your spirit—learn from me.

What would a flower say to me?

Allow each bloom to heal, illuminating God in my fragrance.

Allow eyes to heal in seeing me, as God illuminating in eternity.

Learn how God sees eternity illuminating in you.

Making Us One

Please introduce yourself to readers—not that you aren't totally connected already.
All hello, I am all in the illumination of all.

What is "the illumination of all"?
All is healing, and illumination heals.

Healing illuminates all as illumination allows.

What is "illumination"?
A light alternating in the life-mind in time, healing in God Mind in timelessness.

How do you define "light"?
All electrons and photons flowing into life.

What is the "life-mind"?
A left-brain hemisphere's illuminations.

How long have you been around?
An infinite time in life-mind terms; an instant in God Mind.

What is "God Mind"?
All healed illuminations in the life-mind alternate healed in God Mind. All healed in God Mind is all that is.

Are you love?
All loving, kind, and generous thoughts illuminating both in the life-mind, and in God Mind, making us One.

Do loving thoughts only exist in the present moment, and why you say our 'infinite' is an instant in God Mind?
A healed thought illuminates in God Mind in the instant it illuminates in the life-mind—meaning healing in the life-mind is instantaneous, illuminating in God Mind in eternity.

Does all heal in the life-mind instantly by allowing healed, loving thoughts?
Nothing heals in darkness, only in illumination.

What is "darkness"?
All non-loving thoughts in the life-mind that do not exist in God Mind.

Yeah, that will be our downfall.
All falls in halting love, not illuminating in God Mind.

All heals illuminating in allowing love in the life-mind.

What is "life"?
A holographic illusion allowing God Mind a life-mind illumination to heal.

Are time and space an illusion?
A holographic illusion allowing healing illumination in motioning toward Oneness.

All Heals

Is there a Law of Attraction, LOA?
The Law of Attraction: Halt non-loving thoughts, allowing desires to manifest healed into reality.

LOA could stand for Love of Allowing.
All heals illuminating in loving, and manifests in allowing.

LOA, Lots of Abundance.
LOA, Loss of All non-loving thoughts.

LOL, Laughing Out Loud
LOL, Lots of Love. God is love, healing all non-love allowed by life-minds or not. LON, Love or Not.

HALO How About Love Only
ALOHA, Allowing Love Only Heals All

HELLO Healing Enters Life Loving Oneness
ALWAYS, Allowing Love Will Alter Your Subconscious and conscious manifestations.

Goodbye.
God is standing by.

Waiting for the next loving thought?
I am the loving thought, illuminating in you, if allowing it.

I allow it.
AH! All Heals.

A Healing Dream

I understand that the spirit world has vibration, and our physical world has motion— which requires time and space.
Illusions allowing healing in motion toward Oneness.

A very clever dream.
Dreams always appear to be real in their illuminations, healing the life-mind.

Do we exist in a spirit world that is dreaming of a physical world?
Alternating healing in the physical world, and healed in the spirit world.

What is "the spirit world"?
All that is—meaning all that I am, imagining all that you are.

Am I what you imagine?
A flowing healing, imagined healed, love illumination.

I say that life is temporary, so it can't be real.
A life-mind dream, illuminating illogically in God Mind.

Why do you say that life is a dream "illuminating illogically"?
God Mind illumination is healed; life-mind illumination allows healing—so must not be healed in God Mind.

All not in God Mind is an illusion.

So, that makes me not real, illogically.
*All healed illuminations halting non-love are real,
meaning all love and kindness is real.*

"Get real" would be good to say to myself.
Get healed in getting real.

The love is real, lasting forever in eternity.
Illuminating God Mind eternally, meaning yes.

Is love the only thing that is real?
God Mind illuminates eternally in love, so yes.

What am I doing in a fake, illogical, illusion?
*Allowing it, healing it, illuminating it, and loving all
of it—meaning God Mind halts non-love in you,
illuminating in eternity.*

Getting me to do the dirty work.
*All healing illumination halts non-love, allowing God
Mind illumination in the life-mind, and eliminating
dirty work completely in your mind, if allowing it.*

**That's what the dream of me is doing—healing
my life-mind to know the truth—that I am
really One with God Mind.**
*A glowing, healing, illumination—illuminating healed
in God Mind, and healing in the life-mind.*

*All healed illuminations allowing love are goodness,
meaning Godness.*

The life-mind is my life as a dream.
*A healing dream, illuminating in time and placement,
yes.*

GENEROUSNESS

Is it possible to be too generous?
All generousness means is finally healing into Oneness.

Final healing into Oneness allows flowing abundance in receiving, inversely in multiples of giving.

Multiplying abundance allows more generosity, more healing, more abundance, more generosity, and so on.

How does generosity multiply abundance?
Abundance heals in the life-mind before generous giving.

Generous giving heals in the giver and in the receiver, illuminating more abundance in their life-minds.

Illuminating abundance in life-minds (left brain) heals into the Light Mind (right brain) and opens in God Mind, manifesting in reality—meaning generous giving manifests abundance.

Would selfishness halt abundance?
Abundance is not in line with selfishness; they are not in the same life-mind.

What is the key to being generous?
Live in loving the giving.

Is Godness totally generous?
All generousness is Godness.

How much, and what would a person have to give to be generous?

All according to their gifts and feeling love in their hearts.

NOT A SCALE YOU WANT

Is 'light' the entire electromagnetic spectrum?
All electrons and photons illuminate healing in the life-mind.

If our entire EMF spectrum—from cosmic rays to brain waves—is light, not just the visible spectrum, then we do technically live in a light hologram.
A light hologram projecting illuminations from the life-mind.

Our projections are temporary, so they can't be real.
All holograms illuminate illusions.

Are "illuminations" thoughts?
All thoughts and emotion flowing from the life-mind.

Are life-mind or left-brain illuminations based on judgments, fears, and beliefs?
Beliefs in perceptions, making them illegitimate.

Which makes our projections mostly unsuccessful.
Illogical, halting love, allowing manifestations you do not want.

What are the main illegitimate left-brain projections that are "illogical, halting love, and allowing manifestations we do not want"?

A common illegitimate illumination is that half of all other people are better, and half are not better than yourself.

What is the truth?

All are individual in their illuminations healing, and One in their illuminations healed.

Are they healing or healed in God Mind?

Healing into the Light Mind, or right-brain hemisphere; healed in the Mind of God.

What is the "Mind of God"?

A delicate illumination from the center of your brain, alternating between the left and right-brain hemispheres—also known as the Source Energy, All That Is, the Divine, and Oneness.

Is the Mind of God also love?

All heals in loving life—meaning life loving itself, allowing God Mind to illuminate, so yes.

So our left-brain illuminations are a liability.

Illuminating healing projections into the universe it projects.

Is the universe that I project interwoven with billions of other peoples' universes?

All in an illusion of separation from God Mind Oneness.

As we heal our life-minds, our individual universes heal.
A healed life-mind projects illuminations halting non-loving thoughts and actions, allowing manifestations you desire.

It sounds easy.
Healed illuminations manifest easily; allowing healed illuminations is not easy.

We just need to have peaceful, loving thoughts.
A healed mind allows healed thoughts, illuminating a healed universe.

What are some examples of healed thoughts to focus on?
A healed thought is of love, gratitude, hope, or wonder. Healed thoughts illuminate in the Mind of God.

A healed mind can manifest its desires.
A healed mind illuminates manifestations in God Mind, allowing them into physical reality.

God Mind flows in a peaceful mind allowing love, gratitude, hope, and wonder.

Non-love blocks God Mind flowing and illuminating, halting the manifestations we desire.
Blocking non-love allows manifestations; halting love blocks manifestations.

God Mind illuminates in loving thoughts, or in allowing non-love in life to heal itself.

Everything is on 'a scale from healing to healed'.
A scale illuminating healed in your mind halts non-loving thoughts. Allow loving thoughts and the scale is not needed.

Hating things lower on the scale of non-love does not heal them, it just brings me down the scale.
Flow healed thoughts God Mind illuminates.

And there is no scale.
Not a scale you want to be included in your illuminations.

Gotcha.
God-cha.

Allowing It Is Loving It

How can people always have abundance in their lives? I know people who don't work especially hard or effectively, yet it seems that everything they touch turns to gold, or they always "come out smelling like roses."

The people who "come out smelling like roses" always have loving roses on their minds while they live life in loving it.

Can you please give me a good example of what someone could focus on that would be like "loving roses"?

All might want to focus on God loving them. Heal in life picturing it illuminating in harmony and peace like a rose garden.

Nothing heals in darkness, so picture life in the fragrant garden illuminating in the sunshine.

Silly question, but does God love everyone?
*God illuminates love in life, healing life in time—
meaning life heals in the Light Mind, or left-brain
healing into the right brain in loving life.*

**So God illuminates only love, and people have
to allow it by loving life?**
*Allowing it is loving it. Allowing love into the life-mind
heals each and every manifestation. Allowing healing
illuminates in God Mind, manifesting in life.*

*Not healing in the life-mind does not illuminate in God
Mind or manifest in life.*

All manifesting in life has healed in the life-mind first.

What should our minds not allow?
*All fear in the life-mind allowing judgment, and all
malignant thoughts about others.*

What if others are destructive or selfish?
*Heal them by allowing illuminations to find them,
meaning they will illuminate in the life-mind, healing
into the Light Mind.*

What if they don't allow it?
*Not healing means they will heal in losing their lives,
or in death.*

**It's hard to ignore some of the bad actors on the
world stage, but I have started to.**

All heal in losing their lives or in finding the lightless zone for eternity.[2]

What if they ruin life for billions of people or destroy the planet?
Life heals in loving it or losing it, so either way you will heal.

I will focus on loving the rose garden and not losing it.
All will heal in life, meaning in your manifestations.

So the takeaway is to focus the mind on illuminating what we wish for—blocking out all fear of failure, doubt, thoughts of past failure and regrets, negative judgments of others... basically work on becoming 100% positive, and it will align us with God's energy?
Aligning with God energy means loving life, allowing healing illumination in non-God darkness—healing the life-mind manifestations, opening in the Mind of God, illuminating in eternity.

---

[2] Explained in *Healed in Timelessness* (Infinite Healing trilogy)

Illuminations of Desires

How do our thoughts create our realities?
Loving thoughts heal in the Light Mind (right brain)—half in time, and half in no time—or in timelessness.

Each loving thought healed in timelessness perpetuates light infinitely, meaning illuminating in the healed life-mind (left brain) in timelines on Earth.

Earth lifetimes are healed manifestations, all illuminations of loving thoughts.

You always say to love life and yourself in it.
All loving thoughts heal in the Light Mind.

Healed loving thoughts illuminate in God Mind and manifest in reality—meaning illuminate in the hologram of life.

Let's make an illustration that will apply to a lot of people. Many need extra income. What mental steps would manifest it?
A healed mind does not have needs.

Healing is then illogical if there are no needs.

"No needs" illuminates the logical manifestation of desire.

Illumination of desires manifest in time.

Okay, drop the needy part and illuminate the wish by loving it—and allow it by loving not having needs, and visualize the joyful outcome of our wish?
All illuminates in the loving, joyous visualization—not darkened by doubts or impatient fears.

Great points. Can the visualization be enhanced by placing a bubble around the wish that only allows goodness and Godness into or out of it?
A bubble illuminating love will polish it in the Mind of God.

Polish it? Does that mean purify it?
All illuminations in love are pure.

All polished manifestations highlight detail and glisten in finished condition.

So the wish needs to be detailed?
Delicate, not detailed.

What do you mean?
Delicate means to hold it in your mind lightly.

Like a real bubble or a feather?
A bubble floating into God Mind in your mind.

How can I picture God Mind in my mind?
God Mind in your mind is unlimited, so have it include everything in the universe and increase it infinitely

until you can feel only God Mind illuminating from your eyes.

Allow all that you love to be in all that you see, feel, and do in life.

Would I then be aligned with Oneness or God Mind?
Aligned as One is the natural alignment in all of nature in balance.

Not having balance in nature alters the holistic organism of life.

Life needs energetic balance, or elements need to heal in the organism, creating twoness.

Is that so twoness can heal into Oneness?
All heals into Oneness, yes.

A Loving/Neutral Default

If I am connected to God Mind, I have no needs—only desires that I manifest. So, where does that leave me now?
As a Light Mind healed in God Mind, illuminating in time and place.

Shouldn't I be happier if I am connected to God Mind?
A Light Mind connected to God Mind is not happy or unhappy, it just understands life's neutrality.

I will try to see it that way.
All emotions are healing mechanisms for finding neutral, healed life-mind's layer of lightness in the middle.

Is it good to add feelings to our wish, or do feelings take us either higher or lower out of a neutral position and use too much energy?
All feelings of lovingness heal the flowing manifestation.

What about being joyful—is that the same?
Loving a manifestation illuminates from holding joyful thoughts, so yes.

That would be consistent with Law of Attraction teachings about reaching for higher vibrations, such as joy and love.

A feeling heals in halting non-loving feelings.

Is God neutral?
Neutral in eternal love; not neutral in life-minds.

Unless a life-mind is healed to be neutral?
All life-minds allow love or not, meaning allow God Mind in the life-mind or not.

Allowing God Mind in the life-mind is not neutral, it illuminates in loving life and one's self in it—therefore neutral means loving life only, allowing God Mind illusions to heal in time.

That would be neutral/loving.
A loving, neutral default option.

In a loving/neutral default position, could I manifest what I want?
A loving, polished, imagined God Mind desire always manifests as a neutral default option.

If I desire to manifest major changes in my life—such as moving to a tropical location—how could I manifest that?
A loving, neutral default allows half moving, and half loving not moving, meaning the life-mind default is loving/neutral.

A healed life-mind can then choose a desired option.

What is the key to having this work?
A healed life-mind does not care if it works or not.

Because I am loving/neutral as a default?
Allowing the desired option in time and place.

Should I imagine the option that I choose having specific features?
All features healed in loving neutrality.

Is there anything else I should know?
All features healed in loving neutrality will heal in God Mind and manifest in life.

Is nature loving/neutral as a default?
A default option in all of nature healed in God Mind, yes.

I am visualizing living in a home with tropical charm and a great view.
All will heal in the Mind of God by loving it and allowing it, meaning healing in the home illuminating in your mind opens healed in God Mind.

See you there.
And everywhere.

A Dream of Love and Light

Where is God?
All God flows in holding positive loving thoughts—half in the life-mind, and half in God Mind.

All non-loving thoughts are not in God Mind, meaning they are an illusion.

Are non-loving thoughts an illusion because they only exist in the life-mind which is temporary?
Allowed in timelines to heal.

We allow non-loving thoughts in, but they are illusions that will heal, either in our lives or at the moment of death?
Yes, each in its life-mind in time, or in timelessness.

How could we heal them all in life?
Heal all thoughts, enlightening them in love by acknowledging Oneness in all things.

Allowing non-love means loving it, allowing it to heal in time.

Which requires patience.
All heals holding loving thoughts illuminating it, healing both the giver and light receiver.

Light means darkness cannot exist, or is an illusion.

Are we in a collective dream?
A dream of love and light, meaning non-love is not real.

That makes it easy, I think...
All non-love deals in non-light which is nothing. Love is lightness or the One thing.

That is easier—to focus only on One thing.
Love healing in life illuminates God Mind eternally, meaning love illuminating God Mind perpetuates infinity.

If we were all totally healed, wouldn't there be less light created from healing to illuminate God Mind?
All will become enlightened, or healed in God Mind illuminating in love—meaning illusions of non-love will disappear along with the universe.

Dream over...
Awakened in love in the Mind of God.

Then what?
All will voice its love for itself, meaning the "Ohm" sound—living, healing, and breathing again.

Hearing itself makes consciousness open healing instruments as new universes.

An Elicited Response

What percentage of U.S. mainstream media news on political or world events is either false, deceptive, only partially true, or is totally fabricated?
All of it elicits a reaction in favor of the Hegelian Dialectic instructions that the media conglomerates receive.

All of it is deceptive, and about 30% is not only false, it is misleading. Not all of it is totally untrue.

Not all of it is meant to be misleading, but living in a news event gives certain perspectives only.

Why would they care what a relatively small number of gullible Americans believe?
Altering perceptions in their minds means they live in gullible mind-controlled realities, allowing media conglomerates more control for government and its controllers.

Who does control the U.S. government?
An alien entity that lives in the minds of the most powerful people on the planet.

What would you call the entity?
Many refer to it in terms of the devil, meaning the anti-Christ or anti-God Mind entity in darkness

looking for minds to defile—half in not loving life, and half in not loving itself. Nothing heals in darkness.

I thought there was no devil.
A devil is invited into each mind, meaning allowed in—lowering the illumination to almost nothing in some minds.

Where is the entity from?
A lifeless zone in the far end of the Milky Way Galaxy.

What is "the Hegelian Dialectic"?
An elicited response for perceived events imparted in the media narrative.

Dozens of local news anchors recite the same script.
https://youtu.be/LRAV7h522Ps?si=FjMwcFovZwdEQtLR

How can people create or manifest the lives they want?
All people call their lives into elemental, healing, physical reality—half in their life-minds, and half in God Mind.

All healing in the life-mind opens in God Mind.

God Mind illuminates in the Light Mind—meaning the left-brain hemisphere healing into the right-brain hemisphere—opening life's manifestation.

Allow healing in the life-mind by loving it, not hating anything in it.

Many people can focus on their passion— family, business, hobby—but are also disturbed, or hate to see pain and suffering in the world... often enabled, aggravated, or caused by governments. How should they view these things?
All healing is in the life-mind, meaning all pain and suffering is in the life-mind (left-brain hemisphere of judgment).

Allowing events to heal means not hating them.

The life-mind needs hope, love, and wonder to illuminate healing.

It is hard to accept that pain and suffering are in our minds when seeing whole populations victimized.

All accepting their life-mind's healing manifests illuminations they desire.

All healed illuminations manifest in physical reality.

What if a person happened to be in Lahaina, The World Trade Center, a war zone, etc.?

Allowing themselves to be illuminated in the moment largely meant to ask for spiritual help—meaning from angels, guides, and their future selves.

It would be almost impossible for a person to heal their mind in a war zone or terror attack—so would asking for spiritual help and guidance manifest what they need?

All spiritual requests are answered in an affirmation of God's love for life's creation.

All creation has God listening to it, answering in illuminating healing manifestations.

Does God always answer requests affirmatively?

All requests for illuminating the life-mind, allowing healing in God Mind.

How do we allow healing in God Mind?

Loving the manifestation heals in the Light Mind and opens in God Mind.

If a person is terrified and asks angels, guides, or their future selves for help, would those entities provide the love to manifest the request in God Mind?
All willingly manifest the request—healing it in the Light Mind, opening it in God Mind.

So a person who prays for help will have significantly better lifetime circumstances and manifestations than someone who does not?
All manifesting illuminates in the Mind of God, so listening and talking to God is praying, mainly for guidance in life, so yes.

What is the best way for someone to ask God for help?
Alternate between asking God and asking your future self for guidance.

Ask angels to illuminate the answers in your mind.

And you will always get an answer.
Immediately, meaning instantaneously.

Do our future selves exist, well, in our future?
Illuminating healing in your future—not more than a few seconds in your future.

Then our future selves become our present selves within a few seconds.
Illuminating in the healing life-minds, yes. Picture the future self as a life-mind early warning radar in your aura.

I will, and I'll ask it to wake me up or give me alerts.
It already does, halting injury and harmful incidents.

What is an "aura"?
A Light Body illuminating healing in the Light Mind's holographic projection.

Don't I have a future self that is, say, 5 or 10 years in the future that I could ask for guidance?
A higher flowing self, illuminating in God Mind is a future self, meaning "all that is" is "all that will be."

No comprendo.
Flowing God Mind illumination is all that is. God Mind is your higher self.

God Mind allowing love is all that halts non-loving thoughts, allowing all that the life-mind can be.

A highly illuminating life-mind illuminates a future it desires by halting non-love.

So our future selves would say, *"Love your life now, and the future will be what you desire."*
A healing affirmation that alters future outcomes.

My favorite affirmation is *"I am always in the right place at the right time"*... and it works.
Affirmations motion the highly energized particles in the universe in your favor.

Is that because the affirmation is positive, and doesn't harm anything—so it utilizes God's energy?
Affirming God's energy heals illuminations in God Mind, manifesting in physical reality.

What is the best affirmation?
"All heals in my mind, manifesting in my life in the perfect time."

That is really great, because the mind has to heal to allow the wish to manifest.
"All heals" means the manifestation heals in the mind—opening in God Mind, then manifesting in physical reality, healing the life-mind—making a circular order in the universe.

Starting with a healed mind...
A life-mind healed means the illumination in God Mind is instantaneous.

It sounds like we can heal pain and suffering in our minds instantly—which opens our wishes

in God Mind, manifesting them into physical reality.
All heal in hoping, loving, and wondering how they will manifest.

How will they manifest?
All will manifest in physical reality in perfection.

Because they manifest from God Mind?
A life-mind healed in God Mind means allowing them to manifest.

Would manifestations be blocked or not allowed if there is fear or urgency?
And harming others.

I guess the best wish to manifest would be to have a healed mind and body, and peaceful prosperous days.
All heal hoping that God hears them, and wondering how God loves them.

I already know that God hears them and loves them.
Amen, or so be it.

ALLOW MORE GOOD THINGS

You have hit on the most important spiritual points:

- All non-love or evil does not exist in God Mind, so is an illusion.
- All pain and suffering is only in my mind, doubling down on the illusion.
- Healing is therefore only in my mind.
- My mind heals by seeing only Oneness.
- My healed mind is One with God Mind and manifests my healed illuminations, or what I desire.

All Oneness lives in the God Mind illumination, allowing healing goodness in life-minds open to lightness.

Please explain.
All healing illuminations open in God Mind, meaning highly illuminating in life.

Highly illuminating manifestations—half in the life-mind and half in God Mind—will illuminate in physical reality. Loving the manifestations illuminate more manifestations, and so on.

Is being grateful for every little thing a powerful way to heal the mind and manifest more good things?

Allow more good things, yes.

What does gratitude do, connect us to God Mind?
The healed mind illuminates in God Mind, so yes.

Have I covered it all—non-love is an illusion; only the life-mind suffers; heal the life-mind in Oneness and gratefulness; a healed life-mind manifests its desires?
Loving life manifests more healed illuminations, opening more illuminations, and so on.

I am grateful for your healing information.
All illuminates in God Mind, meaning you are welcome.

Healing Them Instantly

If non-love is an illusion, and people manifest their own realities—I guess there's no point in me watching in horror as they destroy each other.
All heals in life or in losing one's life, meaning in death—healing either way—so no.

Do people attract their own victimhood?
Allow healing in their manifesting non-loving destroyed lives.

All heal in the Mind of God either in time or in timelessness—either in life, or in losing their lives.

Allow healing in them by acknowledging Godness illuminating in them growing brighter in intensity, healing them instantly.

Great idea. Will that improve their conditions since we are One, and they are in fear, etc.?
All heal illuminated in God Mind, meaning healed illuminations manifest for them.

So instead of watching in horror, I will only see the love that allows illumination of their healed manifestations?
And increase the illumination intensity in your mind.

Raising the lightness to God Mind?

All healing illuminates in God Mind, meaning illumination eliminates darkened non-love in their manifesting.

And their lives will improve?
Yes, all healed in the Mind of God cannot improve more than illuminating healed.

Please tell me specifically how to heal people from a distance.
All dis-enlightenment heals in enlightenment. All enlightenment allows God Mind a light opening in a life-mind, meaning it allows God Mind illumination.

God Mind illuminates Oneness—all lovingness, all healing, all peace—allowing healing in life.

God Mind illuminates in your mind, illuminating in all life-minds in their allowing healing.

God Mind is a candle in your mind that lights all candles. Light a candle in the minds of others by visualizing it, healing their life-minds instantly.

Healing life-minds illuminates God Mind, creating more light, and so on.

ACCIDENTS ARE NOT ACCIDENTS

How can people heal past traumas?
All heal in God Mind illuminated, allowing healing forgiveness of non-love or undesirable injury allowed in the moment of non-love, injury, or mindless accident.

Accidents are illogically allowed in each mind open for them.

I know. I broke my foot last year—one day after saying, "I wish I could stop running around."
Actively manifesting the wish.

Does speaking the wish give it more power?
Actively manifesting the vibration, yes.

About forgiveness, or self-forgiveness—it would not be easy to forgive one's self if a person had inflicted serious harm to another, even if by accident.
All will heal illuminated in God Mind as a life manifestation, if requested.

If someone has terrible guilt, should they ask God for forgiveness?
All heals in asking God, meaning all is forgiven instantly.

Will their thoughts about the incident diminish?
Accidents are not accidents, meaning they illuminate wishes healing in the life-mind that invited them.

We probably inadvertently manifest "accidents" and what we don't want all the time.
Allowing the illuminations, yes.

How can we manifest only what is for our highest good—understanding that a broken foot could have been for my highest good?
All manifestations illuminate your highest good, healing the life-mind illuminating in God Mind.

Who knows what our highest good even is?
A big mountain's highest good is to generate "mountain-ness."

Your highest good is to generate God Mind's goodness.

Good.
All good is God Mind goodness.

Here in Maryland they say, "You good."
All allowed in Maryland goodness.

Can you give me an affirmation that people could use to always manifest God Mind goodness, and not any injury or "accidents"?
"Allowing God Mind goodness is my hope, love, and wonder in life."

Western Maryland

ALLOW ONLY LOVE

If evil or non-love is an illusion, and I say it doesn't exist, then it doesn't exist—so I cannot be adversely affected by it, right?
Allowing it illuminates illusions of it.

Hold on—so evil can appear if I allow it?
Loving life illuminates in love, not allowing it.

Allow only love, and only love illuminates in God Mind illuminating in life.

How would I inadvertently allow non-love or evil into my life?
All evil is non-love before it heals in love. Allowing non-love means not healing it.

So, any non-love in myself that is not healed would allow non-love into my life?
Heal non-love illuminating it in God Mind, allowing healing in the life-mind manifestations.

I could use the same earlier affirmation, *"All heals in my mind, manifesting in my life in the perfect time."*
All heals before the life-mind manifests non-love in life.

I need to be really clear on this—if I use the affirmation daily, and practice healing all non-

loving thoughts, then non-love would not be allowed into my life?
A delicate healing illumination means the life-mind opens only in loving thoughts.

Loving life-mind thoughts illuminate life's manifestations.

Healing manifestations illuminate the life-mind.

Healing illuminations open in God Mind, manifesting in reality, and so on.

On a roll, so to speak.
All rolling into time and place as the life-mind allows.

It should be easy but seems like allowing love is our challenge in life.
All heals in life or in losing one's life, so is not challenging.

I guess the question is, "Will I use my lifetime to heal and motion toward Oneness, advancing or achieving my soul's purpose?"
"Will I allow healing in my mind by motioning toward Oneness?" is the healing question.

A healed mind allows manifestation of its wishes, illuminating them in God Mind by loving them in the life-mind.

What would happen to a person's life if they healed their mind by allowing only loving thoughts?

A healed mind would illuminate in God Mind, and allow all desires an effortless manifestation.

And allowing the manifestations would be loving them.
Allowing healing illuminates in loving thoughts, manifesting desires into life.

All healed manifestations heal the life-mind, allowing more healed manifestations, and so on.

Flowing, allowing, receiving.
Healing, illuminating, manifesting.

A Healed Mind Does Not Suffer

What are some other important secrets to manifesting?
All manifestations heal in God Mind before illuminating in the life-mind and physical reality.

Are you saying that the healed manifestations originated in God Mind and not in my mind?
Yes, healing in the life-mind is allowing the manifestation after it heals in God Mind.

God Mind is each person's higher self.

So our higher selves give us the idea of what we want to manifest, and our goal is to allow it?
Yes—heal, illuminate, and manifest it.

Do our higher selves prompt us with ideas of what to manifest because they are for our highest good?
All will heal in God Mind before illuminating them in the life-mind.

Heal ideas in the life-mind by loving them, meaning love all of life, allowing loving manifestations.

Healed manifestations illuminate in physical reality.

As an example, let's say I opened a new business or a store. Assuming it was a good

idea, did my higher self give me the idea to start the business?
Ideas are not all from higher selves.

Allow healed ideas in the life-mind by loving them, illuminating them in God Mind before implementing them.

Love illuminates them or they will not manifest for your highest good.

Ideas that are for your highest good manifest effortlessly.

I have seen that happen in my life— manifestations that certainly had a tailwind, and came together like they were 'meant to be'.
All illuminated in the life-mind and in God Mind simultaneously.

There's the key. How do we know if an idea is illuminating in the life-mind and in God Mind simultaneously?
Millions of healed illuminations have manifested in your life.

All healed in God Mind as illuminations for your highest good.

All "good" means is "God."

If ideas are good, do they go ahead successfully because they are healed in God Mind?
All healed ideas illuminating in God Mind are allowed in the life-mind—healing it, or not.

How do we separate "the wheat from the chaff," or the ideas that are "blessed" from ones that are not?
Illuminations that are loving life allow loving life-mind thoughts.

Loving thoughts heal in God Mind, illuminate in the life-mind, and manifest in reality.

It seems that a lot of bad ideas from non-love also manifest in the world.
All heal in God Mind, meaning they heal in allowing them and illuminating them.

People and the planet suffer though.
A healed mind does not suffer. It half loves life, and half loves itself—meaning in God Mind.

Like nature?
All nature loves life and itself, meaning it illuminates healed in God Mind.

You had once said that "Nothing in nature hates life."
All in nature is healed in God Mind, allowing healing in life, illuminating healed in God Mind.

Talk like that makes me want to live in a bamboo hut.
All healing halts non-love, illuminating healing in the life-mind, healed in God Mind.

Heal illuminated in a bamboo home in your life-mind. 'Home' allows healing illumination in daytime and in nighttime.

Heal illuminating in God Mind in eternity, meaning in no time.

Love in Action

We don't really manifest what we want, we only allow what God wants for us, or not. Is that correct?

Affirming love allows healed, active manifesting in God Mind. Non-love halts active manifesting.

All manifesting is love in action, meaning God Mind in time and placement.

Action means motioning toward Oneness.

God doesn't really want anything, just what we want, or what our higher selves want?

God Mind elicits healing into Oneness, meaning healing twoness.

Healing twoness means eliminating illusions of halting love in non-love.

Non-love is what you call "manifesting what you don't want."

Allowing love illuminates in God Mind, manifesting what you do want.

God Mind is what you illuminate, meaning God Mind illuminates the love in what you want.

God Mind doesn't have needs.

Do our God Mind higher selves know what we want because we chose our challenges or healing objectives before we were born?
Yes, illuminating the most highly advantageous loving manifestations.

Before we are born, when choosing a lifetime healing opportunity, do we see a preview of the lifetime challenges, and not really the achievements?
Mostly loving the challenges chosen—healing in allowing Oneness, illuminating in God Mind.

Sometimes I think that the more challenging a person's life is, the more advanced their soul could be to have chosen the more difficult challenges.
All are allowing love in healing themselves in God Mind, or not healing in life-mind non-love, halting God Mind illuminations.

Do you mean that some challenges could be from life-mind choices rather than from soul level choices?
A healed mind has no choices except loving life illuminating in God Mind.

I think that says it all.
All healing illuminates in God Mind in Oneness. Love illuminates God Mind in loving itself.

That says it all.

Action Steps

I'd like to list some affirmations that people can use. What is an affirmation to heal loneliness?
A healed mind illuminating in God Mind cannot be lonely in Oneness.

Affirm this: "I am illuminating healed, allowing love in my life."

Could that affirmation be used for all of our wishes by adding *"money, health, peace, prosperity,"* etc.?
Yes, illuminations in God Mind heal in the life-mind and manifest in reality.

Because money can be used to sustain us, reduce obligations, and help others—to manifest more money, would I affirm: *"I am illuminating healed, allowing money in my life"*?
All heals in God Mind, meaning illuminates in the life-mind allowing the illumination by loving it.

How can we love a money illumination?
Half illuminate the money in your hand, and half illuminate in loving life's goodness.

Is the "feeling" important—such as feeling the money in my hand, and feeling happy to help others with it?

All feelings of love heal illuminations in God Mind. All healed illuminations manifest in reality.

"I am illuminating healed, allowing money into my life. I illuminate it in my hands and in loving life's goodness."

How's that for an affirmation?

All heals illuminating in God Mind. "All flows into my life in love" is another one.

Should I state a particular amount of money, or illuminate in my mind all the ways I will love partnering with money energy?

Allowing money illuminates all money, healing in life the amount you allow.

Can you walk me through the process—say for a friend who had gotten sick, and now needs to sell his house before it is foreclosed on by the bank?

Action steps to heal illuminations of money are in the following healing steps:

"All will heal in my life in God Mind, and in my mind. Healing in my mind allows my desires to manifest.

All heals in my mind and in God Mind willingly and lovingly by including more than $30,000.

Allowing $30,000 into my life lowers my obligations and my needs, healing all of them.

I love my money healing my mind, illuminating in God Mind—manifesting in my life, allowing my life to heal."

Then should I say, "Thank you, money. My mind is healed?"
Allowing healing in life means loving it.

"Thank you, money. I am loving life—my mind is healed!"
Welcoming it includes it in your life.

"I welcome money to flow through my life like a river, healing wherever it goes."
Illuminating life wherever it heals.

Manifesting Its Reward

Do manifestations flow from God Mind—to be allowed by the life-mind—and then they are received in physical reality?
All filtering in the process.

So we need to clear or open our life-mind filters with only loving thoughts, and to love our wishes, then make necessary preparations for receiving the wishes—kind of like preparing a garden, then planting the seeds, and then loving the anticipation of the garden's abundance?
And loving all of the garden's goodness and life-supporting nutritional benefits.

In this analogy, what is the garden soil?
All of God Mind illumination in the life-mind.

What are the seeds?
All of your healing wishes.

What are the rain and the sunshine?
Love, and allowing love in the garden, healing it.

What is the produce—the vegetables and fruit of the garden?
A healing manifestation from God Mind.

What are the butterflies, bees, and beneficial insects?
All of the life-mind's nurturing thoughts of the wishes.

What am I?
The God Mind garden owner.

Owner and laborer.
Healing in the labor, and manifesting its reward.

LOVE HEALS AND NON-LOVE HALTS

When I think of "the life-mind healing into God Mind," that implies a separation which is not real.

Should I picture them as One with only an illusion of separation created by our life-mind filters?

Is our job to open the filters all the way with loving thoughts of total Oneness, allowing God Mind to flow and not be halted by non-love?
Allowing the mind to heal in loving all of life, meaning loving all in God Mind goodness, yes.

If I witness non-love, is it not in God Mind and therefore an illusion?
All heal in allowing their illumination in your mind.

If I suffer for seeing non-loving events, then my mind isn't seeing the illusion healing.
All will heal in the life-mind's acknowledging Oneness.

Illuminate the illusions with loving, healing thoughts for non-loving illusions to illuminate in God Mind, healing in your mind.

God Mind illuminates the life-mind in loving life, meaning in loving itself opening in the life-mind.

I can only do two things, which are really just one thing:

- see loving Oneness in all of life and goodness
- see loving healing in all illusions of non-love.

Yes, allowing God Mind illumination in your mind.

Does that imply that God Mind is not in our life-minds?
All life-mind is in God Mind, halting or allowing loving Oneness.

So when we talk about wishes that we want, and what our higher selves or God Mind wants, the only difference would be if there are any non-loving thoughts that halt the God Mind manifestation being healed into reality?
Yes, love heals and non-love halts the manifestation.

What kinds of non-loving thoughts would halt a manifestation—fear, doubt, jealousy, greed, etc.?
All of them halt manifesting for your highest good. Fear flows the other non-loving thoughts.

Loving life means not having fear in the illumination you are allowing, or it is not healing in God Mind.

There's a fine line between wishing to manifest money and fearing not having enough.
All heals illuminating enough. In God Mind, "enough" is the loving question.

Loving God Mind enough means the manifestation is enough.

What is "enough"?
Allowing God Mind goodness in life illuminates enough healing in your mind to eliminate fear.

Not eliminating fear means illumination in the life-mind is not enough.

ALLOWING ONLY PEACEFULNESS

I'd like to go over a practical example, using a former neighbor as an illustration.

Let's say I hate how inconsiderate he is. Am I expected to love it and know that it is healing?
It depends how much his life-mind flows inconsideration.

Is it directly proportionate to how much I dislike it?
Yes, illuminations darken in your disliking it.

Attracting what I don't want, and making it worse?
Allowing healing in God Mind makes elemental increases in illumination.

What should I have said to myself when hearing the weekly parties in his new pool right outside my window?
"Allow him his inconsiderations healing in God Mind. God Mind heals my mind, allowing only peacefulness."

What would that do?
God Mind heals illuminations of peacefulness in your mind, meaning the life-mind heals and manifests what it wants.

In that case, I sold our house amazingly fast without even listing it, and we moved away to where I wanted to be.

It was the best move I ever made... better than parting my neighbor's hair with a shovel :)
Yes, illuminating life in another locale meant not healing in a jail.

Definitely.

A Circular Feedback Loop

It's ironic that a healed mind doesn't want for anything, but it can then manifest what it desires.
A healed mind allows all illuminations its higher self manifests for it.

All active manifesting heals; all healing manifests— making a circular feedback loop—illuminating in God Mind, manifesting in life.

What prevents us from instantly manifesting anything we desire?
All heals in God Mind first, meaning that you can.

And I will.
All heals in God Mind. Allow it.

I don't really want anything. What does God Mind or my higher self want for me?
A healed life-mind.

Is that it?
All that illuminates God Mind is it.

I have been working on healing my mind. Have I made good progress?
Almost halfway healed, so yes.

I have noticed life becoming more effortless.

All effort means manifesting needs more healing.

Let's look at another example. What if someone has lost their job, needs a job, or wants a better job in their chosen occupation with more satisfying work?

How could they manifest that?
All healing manifestations illuminating in God Mind will manifest in reality.

Allow healed manifestations by making life's dream job illuminate in their mind, and saying, "This is my healed illumination. I love it, allow it, and live it."

Will the universe then respond and provide the dream job?
Affirming their manifestation healed in God Mind, yes.

Is the goal to have a peaceful mind, or does the mind need to be more in tune with love and Oneness to be healed?
A healed mind highly illuminates loving Oneness— half in God Mind, and half in the life-mind.

How can we do that?
Illuminate loving Oneness in everything eliciting a response—half healing in the life-mind, and half healed in God Mind.

The circular feedback loop is that the universe will respond to my response.

And God Mind is in both responses, depending on what you allow.

Allow love and God Mind is the response.

The Only Response

Let's look at some more examples. I don't watch the news, but on the internet can't help seeing the warmongers and tyrants that we pay for leadership and diplomacy.

How should I respond to my own bitter thoughts?
Allow healing in the life-mind before eliciting a life-mind response.

Find loving healing illumination in acknowledging their healing.

Doesn't that just reinforce the separation as "me and them"?
Healing illuminations heal both giver and receiver in one God Mind loving illumination.

Love in God Mind illuminates all that heals, and all that is healed, meaning one illumination in God Mind.

It's hard to allow in my mind what I'm not willing to accept.
Allowing and accepting heal in their illegitimate leadership roles, meaning their roles in healing the life-mind opening to God Mind.

Are they props to trigger us where we need healing?

All healing elicits a life-mind response. Not eliciting a response is healed in God Mind.

Wow, because a healed mind doesn't suffer?
Not healing in God Mind means love is allowing its response.

Another example. What if someone is betrayed by a friend or a spouse?

How could they heal their mind from the anger and hurt?
Allow healing in the life-mind by loving illuminations of life manifesting what higher God Mind selves activate for the highest good.

Are major challenges scripted for us to respond to or not?
All healing in love is the only response, meaning healing is the only script illuminating in life-minds.

What if a person hates their life—their relationships, their work, etc.?
All can change illuminating healing in the conditions, meaning healing all of the conditions in the life-mind, opening in God Mind. Heal each in the life-mind by illuminating it every evening before sleep.

Affirm, "All heals in my mind, illuminating in God Mind, manifesting my peaceful desires."

Amen.
So be the illumination of it, healed in God Mind.

Karmic Fabric

What if someone is wracked by guilt for being responsible for the death of another person? Are they totally responsible, or is the death agreed upon on a soul level?
All agreeing that healing illumination hastens in dealing in death willingly have participated.

Isn't that a hard way for the survivor to learn?
All heals illuminating in their karmic fabrics.

What is a "karmic fabric"?
A fabric of interconnecting threads all held firmly in place—half illuminating healing in the life-mind, and half healed in God Mind. Depending on the illumination, fabrics come in different patterns, colors, and textures.

Is each thread an individual lifetime or timeline chosen by us?
A "lifeline" to God Mind. Lifelines illuminating in the life-mind heal the fabric.

Then what?
A fabric healed illuminating in God Mind halts illumination of the life-mind, meaning the life-mind no longer exists, illogical as it sounds.

What could a person learn by choosing a life burdened by guilt?
Illuminating healing forgiveness of one's self.

What is a "lifeline"?
Illuminations make lifelines of light, illuminating healing in life-minds. Each life-mind heals in a lifeline from a light source, to a light projected illusion.

Is there such a thing as "karmic debt" where peoples' roles are reversed?
A karmic debt heals illuminating only in the lifeline of the life-mind that chose it.

How much of our lives is predetermined, and how much is determined by our free will and choices?
All healing in life heals in God Mind, healing in each person's allowing it.

Not healing means each person halts God Mind illumination in the life-mind.

Healing in life, or halting in non-love, is determined in each life-mind.

Destiny illuminates in God Mind, meaning Oneness is destined for all.

ALL FINGERS HAVE ATTRIBUTES

Please tell me about manifesting with our hands.

'Mani', meaning 'hand', is the root word for 'manual' and 'manifest' (as I write this 'manuscript').

All manifesting has to do with receiving in the left hand and giving in the right hand.

All fingers have attributes:

- *Left little finger means attachment in an unhealthy way, not allowing manifesting*
- *Left ring finger means holding onto manifestations that no longer serve you*
- *Left middle finger means having the courage in the life-mind to heal itself*
- *Left index finger means to open your mind, healing in God Mind*
- *Left thumb means to illuminate both minds loving life and yourself*
- *Right little finger means non-attachment to material manifestations*
- *Right ring finger means moving the life-mind into lightness*
- *Right middle finger means loving life's lightness*
- *Right index finger means allowing life's lightness to heal all it points to*

- *Right thumb means healing flows into and out of you*

Should we touch the few fingers that have negative attributes with the ones that are healing?
Activating healing in them, yes.

Like a yoga pose?
A healing position illuminating in the life-mind.

I understand that 8 of our fingers send out light, and our 2 middle fingers receive light—and is probably why they are a little longer—to receive more light.
All have elemental light-healing and God Mind manifesting properties.

All heal illuminations in the life-mind—all healed in God Mind.

A healed illumination manifests in reality.

Healing illuminations in the middle fingers will allow God Mind healing illuminations an opening into reality sooner.

Getting closer to an instant manifestation.
Instantly healing in God Mind in no time, healing in the life-mind in time—meaning a nanosecond or more.

What are biophotons?
A biophoton heals illuminating in life, meaning in DNA.

Do biophotons come through our DNA?
Yes.

Where does the light go then?
It projects a universe for you.

Biophotons: The Human Body Emits, Communicates with, and is Made from Light

BY BZ ⊙AM RIGER / 🗓 THURSDAY, 06 MARCH 2017 / ▥ PUBLISHED IN ABILITIES

Biophotons: The Human Body Emits, Communicates with, and is Made from Light

By *Sayer Ji, founder of GreenMedInfo.com*

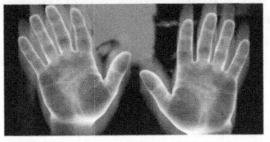

Increasingly science agrees with the poetry of direct human experience: we are more than the atoms and molecules that make up our bodies, but beings of light as well. Biophotons are emitted by the human body, can be released through mental intention, and may modulate fundamental processes within cell-to-cell communication and DNA.

My goodness!
All healed illuminations allowing love are goodness, meaning Godness.

Not flowing goodness darkens DNA portals, halting desired manifestations.

Please tell me about "portals."
A portal illuminates open in life's DNA, or darkens in non-loving thoughts, closing it.

What are portals for?
All portals illuminate the holographic projections allowed by your life-mind, healed into your Light Mind.

It sounds like we want to open the portals that will illuminate the manifestations we desire.
A portal heals open in its illumination of a loving thought.

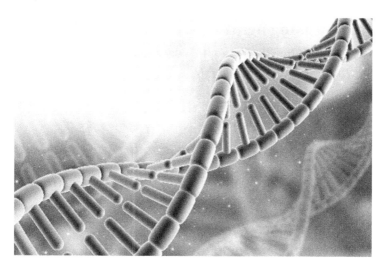

Non-loving thoughts will close our own DNA portals, blocking the light from God Mind, and end up manifesting what we don't want.
A healing affirmation is, "Flowing healing light illuminating from God Mind heals my universe flowing from my mind."

All is well.
All healed illuminations are God Mind living in a universe flowing from you.

God is living in my universe.
A delicate illumination of God Mind—flowing, healing, and perpetuating itself.

THE GODNESS FREQUENCY

Can we open portals to Oneness that are in our DNA by using light?
A frequency of 405 nm, meaning the Godness Frequency, yes.[3]

That is the beautiful blue light that is at the center of our Earth hologram.
Illuminating the life-mind healing in God Mind, yes.

How can we use a laser pointer of that frequency?
Illuminate fingers individually, and middle fingers together while holding your wish in a Flow-er of Life.

Illuminate each manifestation by loving the wish, allowing it to illuminate in the mind.

Manifestations heal in the light, and open in reality.

---

3 See back cover image on left.

Flower of Life

Does our DNA emit light?
All illuminations in the life-mind are illuminating in the DNA.

What are "illuminations in the life-mind"?
A God Mind healed illumination.

Is that why Biblical figures are depicted with a head glow, or halo?
Healed life-minds emit light in open DNA portals.

Everything boils down to healing the life-mind, and it is our main purpose in life.
All heals in life or in losing one's life, so allow healing in life to illuminate in God Mind, making more lifetimes unnecessary.

Heal the mind with light-filled, loving thoughts to become enlightened.
Allow God Mind illumination to enlighten a healed life-mind.

And wear a lampshade hat. Sorry, I couldn't resist.
Laughter heals, illuminating the life-mind—meaning I am laughing, illuminating healing.

I hope I don't manifest a lampshade hat :)
Not now, fears halted it.

I say that God talks to readers of this book, and to all of creation, all the time. What say you?
All allowing my Mind of God illumination, halting non-loving thoughts, yes.

What can people do to hear you?
Allow my illumination into their thoughts by appreciating God illuminating in nature, and in the cosmic design of all that heals illuminating in loving life.

If I illuminate my middle fingers with 405 nm light, does the light travel throughout my body?
All throughout a crystal grid fascia beneath the skin— illuminating healed in God Mind, alternating in the life-mind, meaning illuminating healed in the life-mind.

Do healed illuminations in our life-minds manifest into reality?
Yes, illuminations healed make manifestations real.

Does the light travel from our fingers through our skin fascia to illuminate and open portals in our DNA?
All depending on which portals are intended to open, yes.

Do the DNA portals open by our intentions, and Oneness or God Mind is on the other side?
All healed in God Mind illuminates in open portals.

And they emit light?
Allowing illumination of the life-mind, yes.

So, if I open my DNA portals with light, or loving thoughts and intentions—then God Mind light comes through and heals my life-mind?
Allowing God Mind to manifest all desires healed in God Mind.

What makes our desires "healed in God Mind"?
All in God Mind is healed, meaning all loving desires are healed in God Mind.

If our DNA portals are opened, does God Mind project the manifestation into our minds, which then creates our holographic realities?
A hologram illuminates in the life-mind allowing healed, loving thoughts—activating God Mind, illuminating the manifestation.

If I illuminate my middle fingers with 405 nm frequency laser light, and visualize my wish in a Flow-er of Life healing or turning into light, what happens to it?
A healing in light means manifesting in reality.

I could use the same method in my mind, or with my hands to heal someone's body, correct?
Heal the life-mind and their body will heal.

I would silently ask if it's okay, and should I also ask for their spirit guides or specific angels to help?
All angels will motion on your request—healing, illuminating, and providing love to the request—opening it in God Mind.

When the request opens in God Mind, is it healed?
All in God Mind is healed, so yes.

All is already in God Mind—except our life-mind fears that halt healing and manifesting.
Halting illumination halts manifesting healing. All healing illuminates in God Mind, meaning all healing is not halted in the body, only in the life-mind.

What would an angel look like if I could see one?
Angels appear in different forms allowing them anonymity. Most angels look like half human, and half flying light beings.

Just like what we imagine them to look like.
All depending on images that are imagined.

Have I ever seen an angel in my life?
Angels halt non-love in the life-minds that allow them, and are almost never seen.

You have been helped in many instances, not seeing the angel though.

Angels halting non-love elicit healing—half in the life-mind, and all in God Mind.

DREAMS

We are making wishes and manifesting all the time. Is there a test or a question that we could use to make sure our wish is for our highest good before manifesting it?
All heals in God Mind loving the manifestation, healing it into physical reality.

Ask each manifestation if it has healed in God Mind, or if healing illuminations have halted.

How will we know what the answer is?
All answers illuminate in your mind if asked before going to sleep.

'No' answers illuminate in dreams as fearful images, and 'Yes' answers illuminate in dreams as magical images such as flying.

How can I remember my dreams?
A dream deals in healing emotions. Allow healed emotions to illogically heal the life-mind.

A healed life-mind answers 'No' or 'Yes' in its emotions.

Why is it illogical?
Because logic is not from emotional responses.

If life is a dream—and I am asleep having a dream—is it really a dream in a dream, or did I exit the life dream?
All dreaming in sleep allows the energy body an escape to its home in God Mind.

What does the energy body do in "its home in God Mind"?
It allows the life-mind healing, as the Light Mind illuminates in Oneness.

It takes a break from the illusion of "twoness."
Allowing healing in "youness."

ONLY LOVE

What would you do if you were me? (Trick question since you are me.)
I heal my mind illogically loving, allowing, and flowing only goodness.

Illogically healing my mind logically heals my life, allowing more goodness—meaning more Godness.

It seems that life is just a school where we learn and heal, with the objective of finishing and getting out—not having to repeat it.
A school educating the life-mind by testing illogical healing questions answered by God Mind illuminating it.

The answer is always the same—love it, or allow it and love to see it heal.
Heal it by loving yourself loving it.

What does that mean?
Allowing non-love is loving it. Loving it heals it.

So the answer is to only love—and that is Godness.
Love's healing illumination is Godness, illuminating God Mind in life-minds.

How would you define "Godness"?
All flowing illuminations healing in the life-mind.

What is "God Mind"?
All that illuminates in the life-mind, meaning only love.

Now I know the answer to every test, so the tests will be very easy.
Knowing the answers eliminates testing in the life-mind.

I manifest what is for my highest good, and love talking with God Mind.
Find the method for teaching healing to other life-minds.

How can people best connect with God Mind?
Alternate loving life illuminating in nature, and illuminating God Mind loving, illuminating, and healing as themselves in it.

It seems that the life-mind thoughts and choices are usually wrong, unless they come from God Mind goodness.
All tests that heal in your answer to them.

What else would you like to add?
Loving life illuminates life-minds, healing them open in God Mind.

Allow loving my goodness to illuminate healed in your mind.

MAGICAL MANIFESTATIONS

I trust that all who read this book are far along on their healing paths, and this book will illuminate their minds more.
All reading the illuminating material in this book will halt non-love willingly in their life-minds.

Because their minds are more healed, and you now illuminate in them more?
All heal illuminating in God Mind—half healing in time, and half healed in timelessness.

And the time part is an illusion.
'Illusion' has 'illuminate' in its meaning.

Healed illusions become illogical dreams that logically illuminate in God Mind.

I'm not sure how to respond to that one.
A healed mind elicits a loving response—half in the life-mind, and all in God Mind.

That says it all.
All healed in God Mind illuminating in the life-mind means all has healed itself of illusions.

I will respond with love or neutrality.
Love heals, allowing neutral mindfulness. Not allowing neutral mindfulness manifests what you do not want.

Once the Dalai Lama had said something to the effect of *"Everything is perfect in my world"* — a great affirmation.

All healed in loving Oneness illumination is perfection—half in the life-mind, and all in God Mind—allowing healed manifestations into reality.

That sets the bar pretty high. Most readers have daily pressures from work and family—or from past issues that come up in their minds—myself included. Can they continue discussing them with you to heal them?

Acknowledging God Mind illuminating in their minds alternates between healing in the life-mind, and being healed in God Mind.

Alternating decreases, allowing illuminations to flow healed God Mind manifestations into their lives, magically healing them.

Flowing magical manifestations allow more effortless flowing, and so on.

Will their lives start to improve immediately by acknowledging God Mind in all goodness—and not responding to non-love illusions that are not in God Mind?

All heals illuminations manifesting in perfection, yes.

Perfect.

All illuminates in God Mind loving its own perfection.

That is perfect.

A healed life-mind illuminates in perfect loving Oneness.

Without wearing a lampshade :)
All heals in the lightness of fun illuminating in the life-mind—meaning a lampshade image heals in an absurd illusion, meaning in laughter.

What I want from life's illusion is a healed mind.
A healed mind halts non-love, illuminating healed manifestations into physical reality.

Maybe the word 'halts' should be substituted for 'hates', and 'all' for 'allowing'.
Illuminating God Mind—loving, laughing, and living in an illogical illusion.

Love life and God Mind illuminates.

A God Mind Electron

We discussed affirmations, and also the light frequency for manifesting. Are there other things that would enhance our manifesting abilities—such as stones, oils, sounds, geometric shapes, structured water, etc.?
Yes, all of the above are healed in God Mind, meaning healing in the life-mind.

Which stone is best, or are there many for different applications?
Quartz has the highest life-mind healing property—. allowing God Mind, halting non-love.

What about essential oils?
Frankincense heals in the life-mind, illuminating healed in God Mind.

How about a sound?
"Ohm" illuminates healed in God Mind, illuminating the Earth hologram.

What about a geometric shape?
Tetrahedrons allow healing, having all angles 60 degrees.

Is that the secret of structured water—the 2 hydrogen atoms and the oxygen atom are bonded at 60 degrees to each other?

A hydrogen atom has a God Mind electron in it.

A God Mind electron highly illuminates in contacting and bonding with an oxygen God Mind electron.

What is a "God Mind electron"?
An electron half in God Mind, and half dealing in life-mind illusions.

Are all electrons God Mind electrons?
All electrons are half in God Mind, and half influenced by the life-mind.

Is each life-mind the observer that influences the electron—creating 'The Observer Effect'?
A God Mind electron halts or heals depending on the life-mind observation.

Wow!
A life-mind affirmation healing in amazement.

The implications of that are staggering.
All flows healed into life, meaning love flows and non-love staggers.

Is there a plant, a food, or a flower essence that enhances prosperity?
Coffee beans are abundance multipliers.

How is that?
A coffee bean halts non-love in its illumination. All flower essences halt non-love also.

What Is The Observer Effect In Quantum Mechanics?

Written By Venkatesh Vaidyanathan   Last Updated On: 19 Oct 2023   Published On: 10 May 2019

▶ Table of Contents (click to expand)

> ❝ *Quantum mechanics is the study of how particles at the atomic and subatomic level interact with each other and their environment. The observer effect is the phenomenon in which the act of observation alters the behavior of the particles being observed. This effect is due to the wave-like nature of matter, which means that particles can exist in multiple states simultaneously. When an observer measures a particular property of a particle, they are effectively collapsing the wave-function of that particle, causing it to assume a definite state.*

Let's see, if I want the Observer Effect to work in my favor, do I need to observe love in everything I see?

A healed observer has a healed effect, yes.

Cool.

A cool healing in God Mind electrons.

I will see love in my desired manifestations.

A healing observation makes a healed effect.

God Mind electrons—do your thing!

God Mind electrons halting non-love, illuminating loving manifestations is their thing.

HEALED ANGLES INDUCE GOD MIND

I made a tetrahedron of light[4] using 6-foot garden stakes, white paper, and 2 laser pointers of 405nm frequency.
A healed, elemental God Mind light machine for manifesting.

Would a physical or mental structure like that supercharge healing and manifesting?
All healing is manifesting, so yes.

Do the 60-degree angles and the 405 nm laser light illuminate or open to God Mind?
All illuminate in God Mind, healing in the life-mind, and manifest healed wishes illuminating into reality.

Do 60-degree angles develop consciousness— such as the angles that face each side of a hexagonal bee honeycomb?
All healed angles induce God Mind as healing in itself, meaning all angles that motion toward Oneness.

Is that only the 60-degree angles?
All allow healing or not, meaning 60 degrees is the most illuminating in God Mind.

You had once said that 90-degree angles generate fear.

---

4 See back cover photos, center and right.

All will motion illogically in fear of loving life, halting loving itself.

Illogical because halting love is not logical in God Mind.

Too bad that our living spaces are built almost entirely with 90-degree angles...
Half halting loving life, and half halting loving itself.

What does that do to people living inside of boxed spaces?
Alternates healing and halting healing in life-minds.

I have designed a healing Quonset home structure using all Fibonacci proportions, and it happens to form a 60-degree arc. What would living in that space do for a person?
Allow healing in God Mind to illuminate healed in the life-mind, and manifest life-mind wishes.

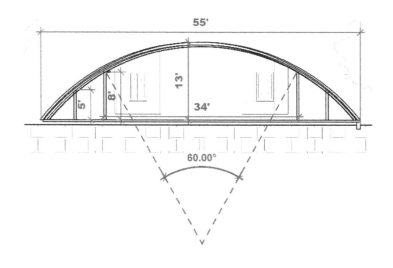

That's awesome—or it will be when built.
God Mind is awesome in its loving life, meaning yourself illuminating itself.

Below is an image of the Bermuda style, but I have different versions for other regions and floor plans.

It is quite economical because the recycled steel shell is the framing, roofing, sheathing, walls, and siding.
All heals illuminating in God Mind, healing life-minds.

I will manifest a home that is healing and comfortable, affordable and attractive, fireproof and termite proof, RF-shielded and made with recycled steel.

What would you call it?
*A home God Mind would love, meaning illuminating
healed in God Mind—to manifest in physical reality.*

**I notice that lines in nature are all flowing, and
it would be pretty hard to find a 90-degree
angle.**

Even the horizon is curved.
*All flowing God Mind is flowing in healing angles that
heal itself.*

*Flowing God Mind illuminates in all angles except 90
degrees.*

Wow.
Flowing illuminates in all other angles.

What is wrong with 90 degrees?
*It illuminates in direct intersections that do not flow
healing.*

You could say that people are the architects of their own manifestations.

Architects hold a vision, allowing it to develop in two dimensions before it becomes a multi-dimensional manifestation.

Do our manifestations need to be thoroughly detailed and thought through?

Architects clearly delineate all of their manifestations in the life-mind before they heal in God Mind.

All manifestations heal in God Mind before a life-mind allows them into their physical reality.

Notice which one comes first—healing in the life-mind before healing in God Mind, then allowing by the life-mind.

We desire something, and it heals in God Mind if our minds are healed—then we allow it into reality.

Architects need engineers. God is the engineer.

A MERKABAH

Speaking of tetrahedrons, what is a Merkabah?
A flowing, healing light-activator.

How do we use it?
A Merkabah has healed God Mind illumination all around it and inside of it.

A healed God Mind illumination manifests in life.

How can we use the Merkabah?
All Merkabah energy has life-mind knowledge illuminating healed all around it and inside of it-healed in God Mind.

Imagine being healed, illuminating inside of one.

God Mind healing love halts non-love, activating life-mind healing.

A Merkabah is 2 tetrahedrons together. Should I picture them spinning in opposite directions? I read that once.
No, hold them half in the life-mind, and half illuminating in God Mind.

Will that heal my mind?
In about a minute, yes.

Should I try to keep my mind clear and only focus on the illumination?

And God Mind healing love illuminating in your mind.

Photo credit: prepareforchange.net

Now, a few weeks later, I have been picturing myself illuminated inside of a Merkabah for a minute each morning, illuminated in the Godness Frequency, 405 nm blue-magenta light. The best way to describe the result is that it seems like my days are perfectly orchestrated. Inside the Merkabah, all of the 8 angled points of 60 degrees would be pointing at me, correct?

All halt non-love in your life, meaning they illuminate it in love.

A Merkabah illuminates God Mind in your mind allowing healing illumination.

Is it the combination of geometry and light that heals my aura or Light Body, that heals my mind?
A combining of the life-mind allowing healing, and a Light Mind illuminating healed.

All illuminating in the Godness Frequency and in a Merkabah, circle in a feedback loop into God Mind healed, and into the Light Mind healed.

The perfect place to be.
A life-mind enlightening place to be.

A Candle in a Dark Room

Isn't it 'whistling past the graveyard' to be focused on God Mind and not in the life-mind?
Allowing God Mind healing in the life-mind illuminates in God Mind and in the life-mind, healing the life-mind.

The life-mind healed illuminates in God Mind, allowing God Mind to flow healed manifestations illuminating in life—meaning non-love halts in your life-mind reality.

Gotta love that.
Halting non-love means love illuminates—half in the life-mind, and all in God Mind.

Win-win. Obviously, letting myself get dragged down will not raise anybody else up.
It will lower the average vibration for all, and halt flowing healing illumination for all.

How does keeping my consciousness high help others?
It allows everyone else illumination, becoming a candle in a dark room.

Which gives them light—from which they can light their own candles.
A candle in a dark room has one purpose—to illuminate it for all.

I do love that.
Acknowledging love heals the life-mind, lighting the candle.

Loving ourselves is loving life and loving God.
All healing in each life-mind is healed in God Mind, meaning illuminating God Mind as yourself.

God loves me, meaning God loves itself as me.
God illuminates as each person loving life, healing itself.

I have concluded that watching the news will ruin your day, and watching it every day will ruin your life.

Have a loving/neutral default response, and be vigilant to stop mental disturbances and negative thoughts with focus and discipline.

The desires of our peaceful minds illuminate healed in God Mind, manifesting in reality.
Allow healed manifestations into your life.

Give God Mind thanks for illuminating in the life-mind.

Accept all gifts illuminating God Mind goodness.

Thank you, God Mind, for this book.
A book half illuminating in God Mind, and half in each reader's life-mind—healing their desire for mind healing, illumination, and manifesting goodness.

Will you come through each reader's peaceful, loving thoughts?
As God Mind illuminating healed, yes.

I will focus on your coming through, and nothing else.
All healed in God Mind means there is nothing else.

Just illusions.
Allowed in life to heal.

If we raise our consciousness to a higher vibration, does it flow outward like electromagnetic radiation and keep lower vibrations away?
Flowing healing outward like light, yes.

Each light photon has in itself a God Mind illumination light particle acting in the life-mind, and in God Mind.

And the particles respond to our peaceful, loving thoughts?
Manifesting your life-mind healed wishes, yes.

Do our intentions activate them into a wave state from a particle state?
All healed in illumination in both states.

Are we then connected with God Mind?
Allowing God Mind illumination.

Some people have told me that they are not spiritual. What would you say to them?
All elemental life illuminates in a hologram, meaning life is not physical.

Elements heal in the life-mind, illuminating in God Mind—making their illuminations healed God Mind inflections of love.

Healed inflections of love illuminate half in the life-mind, and all in God Mind—illuminating the life-mind's healed manifestations.

What would you say to someone looking for confirmation on the existence of God?
Only "Hello, healing one." Healing illuminates healed in me, so "Hello, illumination!"

Life is a school—and we will learn either the easy way, or the hard way.
Always learning, healing in illumination.

What are we supposed to learn?
That life is God Mind healing itself in life-minds, illuminating in eternity.

God Mind allows life-minds freedom in their choices, made in a linear timeline on Earth.
Millions have healed in their lifetimes, and billions have healed illuminating in losing their lives.

Losing one's life means illuminating healed in God Mind.

Have only a fraction of people healed their life-minds?
About 5% heal illuminated in life-minds.

That's a lot.
Healed illuminating, not enlightened.

What does it take to be "healed illuminating"?

All fear of life and death has healed, illuminating in God Mind.

Are animals "illuminating healed in God Mind"?
All plants, animals, and microorganisms.

They are good teachers. Life on Earth is a hard school, even with all the teachers.
The life healing school is getting harder because life is getting harder in halting non-love in life-minds allowing it illogically in. Not allowing non-love in the life-mind is logical—healing the life-mind, illuminating in God Mind.

As stated before, life-minds are allowed freedom in their choices.
Allowed to heal or not heal in life. Not healing in life means healing in losing one's life, or in death.

Then you end up not graduating—and coming back to school for more pain in another lifetime.
And more healing lessons, yes.

How can I learn the easy way to graduate?
Heal the life-mind's illogical maligned thoughts by allowing non-love to heal, and loving life illuminating healing in itself.

I think of animals as healed beings.
Illuminate in your animal nature.

Specifically, I was thinking of a peaceful Crow.
Live illuminating the Crow's mind allowing healing in itself.

Is that my totem animal?
For you, meaning each person has their own.

Will it help a person to heal their mind if they identify with an animal?
Animal or plant, meaning trees or flowers.

Do we have more than one totem, or is that something we choose?
Choosing one illuminates in your mind in that moment, meaning it chooses you.

Crow

Is there a frequency for prosperity?

Frequencies allow God Mind a highly illuminated opening into life-mind manifestations, meaning they illuminate God Mind in the moment of healing the manifestation—half in the life-mind, and all in God Mind.

Love illuminates in number 8

Empathy illuminates in number 5

Compassion illuminates in number 9

God Mind illuminates in numeral 1

Acceptance illuminates in number 4

Altruism illuminates in number 2

Courage illuminates in number 3

Malignment illuminates in number 6

and all halting love illuminates in number 7

So there are 8 positive and 2 non-positive numbers.

All are highly illuminating. Not illuminating much are numbers 6 and 7.

Please explain.

All numbers have highly illuminating properties except 6 and 7, maligning them in the number 13 together.

The number 13 has a magical meaning, illuminating in knowledge healing life, magically illuminating it—half in the life-mind, and all in God Mind.

I just counted 13 points on my Metatron coaster.
Will Metatron illuminate healing knowledge in you?

"Yes," Metatron says.

Metatron

Metatron, or Matatron, is an angel in Judaism, Christianity, and Islam mentioned three times in the Talmud, in a few brief passages in the Aggadah, and in mystical Kabbalistic texts within Rabbinic literature.

How do I use different numbers to enhance my life?

All illuminate healing in your imagining their logical influences in life, meaning imagining their attributes in the numbers.

Healing illuminates in their imagining instantly.

I just looked at the clock, and it happens to show 1:11. Is that the best repeating number series?

All heals illuminating in God Mind, so yes.

What else do I need to know about numbers?

Healing in 111 is the most illuminating. Healing in 456 illuminates in allowing empathy illogically, and so on.

Are there special attributes to long numerological sequences?

All heal illuminating in their attributes.

Once I was doing a presentation in a bookstore, and for an employee there, I changed his frequency to "the frequency of prosperity." He won a lottery jackpot 3 weeks later.

All healed illuminating his frequency to prosper at the time. He lost monetary gains in illuminations darkening.

Did I change his frequency by non-verbally sending him a message that he is attuned to prosperity?

DNA portals opened, flowing healing prosperity, activated by your dowsing.

All frequencies come from the life-mind, so his allowed healing that had been sent by you.

Did he close the prosperity portals soon after?
All of his decisions halting love closed them.

"Prosperity" could mean different things— money, health, satisfying work, more time with kids, etc.
All healing illuminations mean prospering.

What is the number for monetary prosperity?
Allow healing in 549.

I'll set my phone to beep at 5:49. Maybe it also has an "Ohm" sound :)
Allow healing illumination in the numbers illuminating.

Is there a number for healing the body?
All illuminate in the life-mind, healing in the body.

Is there a number for improving one's business?
11 heals life-minds in business activities.

Finding a loving partner?
1 illuminating in the number 2 heals in loving partnerships, logically.

Healing the mind?

Hold open illuminations of number 1—healing in the life-mind, opening in God Mind, logically.

1 is for Oneness. What does number 10 mean?
All illuminations in the life-mind are healed in God Mind.

What is another significant number to use?
All illuminate healing in the life-mind; maligning numbers 6 and 7 illuminating less.

Heal the life-mind illuminating the highly illuminating numerical attributes.

Can each letter in the alphabet be assigned its corresponding number, then the number sequence be used in place of the letters, such as L-O-V-E is 13 + 16 + 23 + 6 = 22, then 2 + 2 = 4?
Love illuminates in number 8, so no.

Does God have a favorite number?
One and one makes you.

A Home in God Mind

In my book *Poems and Messages for the Loss of Your Animal Companion*, you said that you promised animals "a loving home in nature, or lesser degrees of living in a home with people." What is promised to people?
A home in God Mind if they choose illuminating thoughts.

Would our lives on the planet be a lot better if our thoughts chosen were all illuminating?
Allowing God Mind illumination is always better for the life-mind, healing in God Mind.

Because we can manifest our desires, and not be adversely affected by other peoples' manifestations?
A healing illumination does not adversely affect anyone.

Are you saying that there are only healing manifestations?
All healed manifestations are illuminating in God Mind. All healing manifestations allow healing in God Mind.

Either way, healing illuminates in God Mind.

What if I was walking down the street and a bomb landed near me? Would that be my manifestation?

A life-mind experience that illuminates healing in God Mind—immediately in life, or instantly in losing one's life.

If my mind was healed, would I have been walking on another street, or at another time?

A healed life-mind moves effortlessly, illuminating half in the life-mind, and all in God Mind.

Does "moves effortlessly" mean that avoiding a bomb would not be necessary?

All effort flows from not flowing effortlessly. A healed life-mind flows effortlessly.

A bomb halting love means that non-loving effort in life-minds is allowed into your life.

I thought we are supposed to be neutral and allow non-love to heal.

All heals illuminating in allowing it. Allowing it healing eliminates it in your life.

Better to eliminate it than to illuminate it.

Healing non-love eliminates it; all healing in love is illuminated.

So, if my mind ranges on a scale from neutral to loving, would my life become effortless?

Effortlessly healed in God Mind, yes.

Is that what is meant by 'non-judgment', to not judge things as good or bad—just healing?
Healed, or allowed to heal, yes.

The implications of that are flowing...
Illuminating healing in God Mind, flowing in the life-mind.

That's the biggest bombshell so far, not sure if a pun is intended.
Healing illuminates in a bomb or a flicker.

So all is good then.
All illuminates in God Mind goodness, allowing the life-mind God Mind illumination.

Do you have an affirmation to use for being non-judgmental?
"All heals illuminating in God Mind."

Accidents are not accidents—so there are no victims?
Illumination in God Mind means all are winners.

Will every reader who is drawn to this book heal their mind significantly, and manifest their desires more effortlessly?
Effortlessly, not "more effortlessly."

For Your Highest Good

Life is like a game of golf—focus on your own game, and keep your eye on the ball.

Don't try to hit someone else's ball.
All carrying their own clubs makes it fair.

Good point. If someone is better at the game and manifests effortlessly, it would be like having no sand traps, ponds, or rough areas to play between.
Healing on the green, having mastered the game.

What would you add to the golf analogy?
Golf clubs are life-mind thoughts illuminating in their swings.

Golf balls allow healing manifestations illumination in life.

Holes in the green are your objectives in life.

The clubhouse means illumination of leisure.

Translation: "Good thoughts allow manifestations to reach your objectives effortlessly."
All healed in God Mind, illuminating in the life-mind.

How long would it take a reader of this book to manifest like a 'golf pro'?
About 15 hours with practice.

Bobby Jones

What is the best way to practice—use affirmations, be mindful of thoughts, be grateful, etc.?
And heal the life-mind, illuminating in God Mind imagining a Merkabah light machine around itself— flowing illumination in God Mind.

I just had an idea. What if I bought or made a small wire Merkabah and put a picture of myself in it, and illuminated it? I could try making a big one with golf clubs but would be kicked off the golf course:)
A mental one heals as well as a model.

Do the magical points of 60-degree angles of the Merkabah heal our minds and our wishes?

*Illuminating both in God Mind, flowing the life-mind's
healed wishes into reality.*

**I am picturing the healed life-mind opening
portals in my DNA—like flowers or a filter—
opening to Oneness illumination on the other
side.**
*Allowing filters of non-love to heal open in the Mind of
God, illuminating the life-mind manifestations into
life, healing the mind.*

**For a wish to be healed, does it have to be for
my highest good?**
All healed manifestations are for your highest good.

**As an example, a wish for winning the lottery
could disrupt my life and relationships, but if
my mind was healed, I wouldn't care if I won or
not. What would be for my highest good—
winning, or not winning?**
*All healing halts non-love, meaning the lottery
manifestation illuminates or not.*

A healed manifestation means not having disruptions.

**Great point. I would have to be at total peace
with winning or not winning—to illuminate
either one as my healed wish.**
*Loving the manifestation means holding it in the life-
mind illuminating, so illuminate the one you desire.*

Aces in Your Hand

I understand that we make Life Agreements on a soul level before we are born.
Agreeing illuminations allowed in life will be healing the soul's purpose of knowing the God Mind instructions of loving itself.

Will a soul only make agreements that it can keep?
Agreements heal in their initial inceptions, illuminating in God Mind—meaning that they are manifestations that heal life-minds—allowing more manifestations, healing the life-mind, and so on.

Like playing the hand you are dealt, in a game of cards.
All cards chosen in life illuminate the next hand to play.

Do we choose the game before we are born, and then choose the cards continuously after we are born?
A few Aces are in each hand, meaning each play can be the one you want to manifest.

Each person has a few 'Aces up their sleeve'.
Halting non-love will make all Aces in their hand.

Deal me in.

Allow healing in the dealing.

That's my feeling.
Aces revealing; non-love reeling.

Good one. If each card is one of our thoughts, we can choose any card from 2 to 10 and higher—including Aces.
Each card illuminates in the higher suits—meaning Jacks, Queens, and Kings.

I don't play cards, or golf.
A game heals illuminating in the life-mind, meaning the game of healing that you cannot lose—only heal.

Especially if I kept drawing Aces.
Healing illuminates in each hand—illuminating healed in Aces.

Illuminating healed means God Mind holds Aces in your hand.

Allow God Mind to play.

A HEALED UNIVERSE

On another occasion, you said that inside each of our DNA portals is a universe.
A healed universe illuminating your desires, healed in God Mind—allowed into life by the life-mind.

Filaments illuminate, healing the portal open.

Just like a flower opening in sunlight?
A flower heals illuminated in the light. Each flower has filaments in its center flowing life, meaning pollen that allows more life to illuminate in life.

What are "filaments"?
All filaments highly illuminate the Earth hologram, allowing Earth healing illumination from each life-mind's projection.

Are filaments in our minds?
All filaments are in open DNA portals, illuminating in the life-mind and God Mind at once.

What does a filament look like?
A light bulb filament, meaning an illuminating coil—half in the life-mind illuminating healing, and all in God Mind illuminating healed.

Are our DNA portals opened by thoughts of loving life, and closed by all negative thoughts?

All thoughts either open or close portals. An open portal illuminates in life, meaning all healed open portals allow new universes to illuminate in reality.

Let's say I had a negative thought about my former neighbor. It would close portals in my DNA, and then what?
All healing manifestations are halted.

All of them?
All healing illuminations are halted in closing DNA portals.

Wow, that can't be good.
All heals in goodness illuminating; all darkness halts healing illumination.

My neighbor may have been attracting it though...
All manifesting healing illumination in life manifests in your life only.

His life-mind manifests or not, depending on his thoughts only.

There is the Oneness and separation conundrum. I am one with life and other people, but their manifestations have absolutely no impact on me?
All healing illuminates in your mind, illuminating in God Mind, or in Oneness.

Halted illuminations do not exist in God Mind.

So if I flow only healed illuminations as my thoughts, there won't be any major annoyances in my life?
All annoyances heal in God Mind, illuminated by allowing them and loving life.

And they will go away?
Or you will, yes.

Into a whole new universe.
Created, healed, and illuminated for you, and by you.

Financial Filaments

Can you please tell me how to manifest financial independence?
Allow healing in financial filaments by illuminating each of them with a life-mind filament of loving them.

Financial filaments are highly illuminating in your life-mind hoping for illumination.

What is a "financial filament"?
A delicately illuminating God Mind elemental holographic engine illuminating the hologram.

Where are they?
All filaments heal illuminating in life-minds.

Can I illuminate them by loving them?
Healing illuminations will activate them, manifesting them into reality.

How many financial filaments are there?
About 50 or 51 depending on the life-mind.

Could you please give me a few examples of them?
Filaments of accepting money, detaching from money, flowing healing illuminations with money, flowing bill paying obligations, and so on.

Besides loving the financial filaments, can they also be illuminated another way?

All filaments illuminate healed in your loving them, manifesting your desires.

I am going to illuminate them by shining a 405 nm laser on my middle fingers, while holding the intention that my financial filaments are healed.
A God Mind frequency for illuminating filaments heals all of them, illuminating them in God Mind.

What should I expect if I illuminate all of my financial filaments using a 405 nm laser?
A healed financial illumination of your financial desires.

When I first learned from you about healing and manifesting with light, I illuminated my middle fingers (as described above) while making a wish for prosperity. The very next day, I was awarded 2 huge projects, that were 10x larger than my typical projects.

Only one job went ahead and I completed it successfully. It would have been too much to have both at the same time anyway. My friends had similar successes.
Asking heals, allowing feels, accepting seals.

Good deal.
Making deals in the life-mind real.

It seems that the 405 nm laser method is the sure-fire way to illuminate filaments, open portals, and manifest our desires.

Fire heals in illuminating and purifying.

I used the same 405 nm light method to manifest a specific large amount of money. Over the next 5 months I made 1,000% trading commodity futures—gaining the exact amount I had wished for... then lost 1/3 of it.
Allowing it healed it, and fear of losing it lost it.

Flow healing into allowing your manifestations.

I noticed in this book that the word 'deserve' is not used. We manifest what we 'desire' rather than 'deserve'.
A desire illuminates all healing in allowing deserved goodness.

Do we deserve goodness?
A flowing, healing lifetime of goodness, yes.

Will you provide it?
All flowing, healed illuminations are God Mind healing light—meaning all will flow if allowing illumination, halting non-love in your life-mind.

If we halt non-love in our minds, then do we deserve goodness?
A desire heals, illuminating in its deserving it.

I will reserve it.
Allow God Mind to serve it.

No need to conserve it.
I can preserve it.

THE HEART MASTER PORTAL

How do we manifest through our DNA portals?
All open portals illuminate healed in God Mind.

God Mind illuminates in the Heart Master Portal, meaning God Mind is illuminating in you.

To what degree?
To the degree each person illuminates loving, peaceful thoughts.

Healed manifestations in the Heart Master Portal accelerate in subatomic activity for the manifestation to be realized in life.

Is the Flower of Life in our hearts?
A Flow-er of Life is in each Heart Master Portal.

What else can you tell me about the Heart Master Portal?
A Heart Master Portal heals the life-mind or not, depending on how much it illuminates on opening.

Illuminate it loving life.

Heart Master Portals heal the life-mind, illuminate in God Mind, and allow life to heal in life.

What if I chose all loving thoughts—about others, about myself, about my desires, about non-love in the world that needs healing?

All heal in God Mind and illuminate in realizing their healing.

A healed thought illuminates in God Mind, and calls forth the light in the universal hologram to illuminate in your Heart Master Portal.

Holy cow! I mean holi-gram. Please explain that.
All light illuminating the hologram illuminates in your Heart Master Portal, allowing healed illuminations in life.

So our thoughts are projecting our entire universes?
Illuminating them, yes.

Holy cow again. Do we each live in our own universe? I think I know the answer to that.
A light hologram can only be illuminating from a light source in each life-mind, illuminating God Mind in each life-mind healed manifestation.

Life-mind heals or not—illuminating in life, or not.

All life-mind healing illuminations are healed in God Mind.

Life-mind illuminates God Mind in its own hologram.

We just need to get out of the way—and not block it with fears, judgments, beliefs, etc.
Allowing means not having illusions of life that are non-loving.

Let's say my thoughts were all in the light—not having "illusions of life that are non-loving."

Would God Mind illuminate in my Heart Master Portal and project out to organize the entire universe?
Healed illuminations halt non-love in your universe, meaning the life-mind's healed universe, so yes.

I'm still trying to grasp the implications of that.
Life-mind grasping loving thoughts heals the entire life-mind universe, illuminating the implications.

It's pretty complex for all of our universes to be intertwined, with each manifesting only for itself.
Infinitely complex; healing them is simple.

Do our healed thoughts make subatomic reactions that project out from the Heart Master Portal, and influence the entire universe?
All healed God Mind thoughts are the hologram, illuminating the life-mind in God Mind—making the hologram illumination in your mind.

So, life really is a dream.
A dream of love—or non-love, making it a nightmare. Dreams allow healing.

That is all very empowering—that we each have total control of our own universes—just with our thoughts.

An illumination healed in God Mind, yes.

Any non-loving thought is not in God Mind, so it bumps us into an unhealed universe that we don't necessarily want to be in.
All healed illuminations are in God Mind, all unhealed illuminations are not in God Mind, meaning they are an illusion.

How about this for an affirmation? *"I am healed in God Mind, since losing my illusions."*
"Allowing illumination of my manifestation" will complete it.

Is there a code we could use to manifest our desires?
A God Mind code illuminates in all loving affirmations and thoughts.

What is the code?
A light, highly focusing in life—meaning God Mind illuminating in loving affirmations and thoughts.

Love makes a light code.
A code illuminating God Mind in your mind—healing, illuminating, and flowing all of the life-mind's desires.

ALL THAT WILL BE

I think of the Heart Master Portal as like a Star Trek Transporter Room, with a Flow-er of Life design on the floor.

I visualize my wish on it turning into blue-magenta light, The Godness Frequency.

The wish heals in God Mind, and manifests into physical reality.

A light healing transporter of loving intentions, healed in God Mind, allowed to manifest in reality.

How does it work? As soon as I visualize my wish turning into light, is it instantly healed and in God Mind?

Yes.

Is that because the frequency is love?

A God Mind frequency illuminating in love, so yes.

Then do I only have to allow it into reality?

Yes, allow it to flow into your life.

Should I open DNA portals to allow it, or are they for projecting it out?

All portals open to God Mind illumination, meaning they open illumination flowing "all that is"—or God Mind goodness—into "all that will be." All healed desires are "all that will be."

Are my desires healed by visualizing them turning into 405 nm frequency light?
Yes.

My manifestations are "all that will be"- not just specific desires, but every moment of my life will be healed and allowing, abundant and prosperous, safe and protected, etc.
All flows illuminations of God Mind from your mind, healed into all time, allowed into one lifetime.

Well said. I don't just allow it, I invite it.
A life-mind invitation in God Mind accepting it.

Welcome to my dream of love and light... and illusions to heal.
My invitation says 'Black-tie or costume only'. I can be 'The Invisible Man'.

Groann...
All heals in the absurdity in laughter.

MATCHES MADE IN HEAVEN

I had a not very honest client who was short-changing me for my work. If my mind was healed, would I not have attracted him—or would the healing thought have been, "I want the best for you, but love myself and want the best for me"?

All clients form relationships healing both involved. Highly illuminating life-minds attract highly illuminating clients.

And they both manifest together.

All healing in their life-minds, and in their businesses.

A match made in heaven.

Matches made in heaven, illuminating in reality.

Matches lighting candles.

Matches lighting illuminations healed in God Mind.

A few weeks ago, I got sprayed by a skunk while trying to get the dogs away from it.

They learned their lessons. What was my lesson?

All heals in natural illumination of the skunk's smell, healing in motioning away from it.

Kind of like moving away from my former neighbor?

Illuminating manifestations of what you want, yes.

Instead of having to choose the right school, the right job, the right partner, house, or car... we just need to choose the right thoughts— peaceful and loving, correct?
Allowing God Mind manifestations of the right illuminations.

Is it fair to say that God or "the universe will decide" if we get out of the way?
The life-mind allows God Mind illuminations, yes.

But we still have to act.
The life-mind can act or not—healing manifestations, or not.

Allowing healing is also an action.

DISTILLING ALL OF LIFE

Back to my earlier example: How could I be one with my former neighbor? It seems like it would be mixing dirty water with dirty water, and saying it is still water—but God Mind is the pure water.
All healing in the purification process, allowing distillation of the pure water.

We are all one—either healing or healed.
Yes, healing in life, allowing God Mind—or not.

I just need to know how to be highly functional in a highly dysfunctional world—among the people anyway.
All functions allow loving thoughts or not.

All functions illuminate healed in God Mind as loving thoughts.

All functions manifest—half in the life-mind, and half in God Mind—highly functioning and illuminating in your life.

Dysfunction halts illumination in life, meaning dysfunction halts manifestations.

Halting manifestations makes more dysfunction, and so on.

So, I need to have a loving/neutral response to every thought for my life to function optimally, and other people can function or dysfunction however they think.

A function of God Mind heals life by loving all of life, healing itself. Healing itself means distilling all of life into one healed thought, "All heals in my mind; all is healed in God Mind. I love all of life healing me."

I love the distillation metaphor. That boils it all down, yuk, yuk.

Allowing love to surface healed in God Mind.

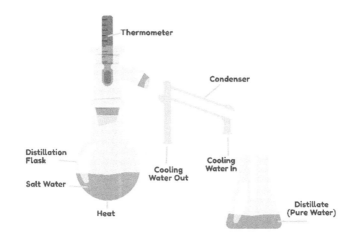

That is where we want to be—and from there we can simply manifest our desires.

All healed in God Mind manifests in reality.

The best part is that if I am immune to inconsiderate neighbors and the rest of

dysfunctional humanity, I won't attract their dysfunction, correct?
All enters into the graceful, healed world God Mind intends for life, including yourself.

I can't wait—well, I'm not going to wait.
Already healing the life-mind.

"...enters into the graceful, healed world God Mind intends for life..." That says it all.

That is our challenge, and you would think it should be easy.
Just a matter of allowing what is flowing—and receiving it.

ILLUMINATION HEALS YOUR FUTURE

Do you have any jokes?
What do flowing, healed God Mind manifestations look like?

All that heals in your good looking.

Ha! Good looking, loving, and living.
God loving in your loving and living.

God a-loving in my allowing.
God a-loving and a-living in your allowing.

Living and a-loving and not a-losing.
A-losing illusions illuminating in a-loving.

I'm a-laughing.
All heals in God Mind a-lighting a-laughing.

A laughing Buddha comes to mind.
Buddha is enlightening God Mind in laughter.

Photo credit: laughingbuddhabuzz.blogspot.com

139

We can manifest only in the present moment with our thoughts, correct? Thoughts about the past need to be instantly healed with forgiveness, and thoughts about the future need to be our peaceful wishes.

A healed mind illuminates in God Mind and manifests its wishes.

Does a healed mind stay in the present moment?
All love illuminates in the present moment, so yes.

Could I heal the past in the present moment by forgiving it with love?
All heals in the moment of illumination, meaning illumination heals your future also.

Now we're talkin'.
Now we're illuminating.

Now I'm manifesting what I desire—key word 'now'.
Healed God Mind illuminates now in eternity.

Always now.
Always illuminating.

Always manifesting our desires.
Always if allowing the illuminations.

When you say "illuminate," do you mean having loving thoughts?

Illumination heals—meaning it illuminates in God Mind, allowed in the life-mind as loving, healed intentions—so yes.

If I forgive my past in the present moment, and it heals my future—does that mean it heals everything else after it that is still in the past, or does it heal me in the present moment, which heals my future?
Healing in all timelines, illuminating in the present moment.

What does that do?
Healing in all timelines means all DNA portals that are closed in the past, are now open in the future, and in the past.

All opening in the past heal in God Mind, altering the past—illuminating other universes.

All healed in God Mind illuminates a life-mind universe that you desire by allowing it.

Does that change us now on our linear timelines?
All healing in the life-mind halts non-loving thoughts, allowing God Mind goodness and manifestations you desire.

So, if we forgive ourselves for all the times we were not loving, kind, or generous—it would heal our regret or guilt which have closed portals in our DNA.
Healing illuminates in the Mind of God instantaneously.

LIGHT HAS NO SHADOWS IN IT

What I often do mentally to set an intention is visualize a bubble of protection around myself, my car, family, business, house, etc. It protects them, correct?
All visual intentions manifest in their allowing healing in their imagining.

I could also use a bubble of prosperity.
A bubble healing the life-mind is a God Mind balloon— illuminating half in God Mind, and half in the life- mind.

One year ago, a good friend was about to give up selling his house, wishing he had listed it for sale months earlier before interest rates had doubled, peoples' kids went back to school, etc.

I suggested that he picture a bubble around his house that would "attract the right buyer at the right time."

The next day he got two offers! The higher offer was for tens of thousands of dollars above the asking price. He texted me at that time that my mental trick worked. In the same transaction he and his wife bought their dream home. They still can't believe it.

All healed illuminating in God Mind—allowed, illuminated, and healed in the life-mind.

God Mind illuminating in the life-mind is the balloon, inflating the life-mind's healing manifestation.

What would happen if I expanded a balloon of truth, love, and peace around the whole world?
All life-minds heal if allowing it.

How about a balloon that also says, "Allow this"?
All heals illuminating in God Mind, meaning the life-mind heals if healing is allowed.

Healing illuminates allowing, so about 15% of life-minds heal in the bubble, allowing it.

Wow! The implications of that are flowing.
All healing allows flowing, meaning God Mind flows in life-minds.

The non-love would be staggering.
Not flowing love is halting and not even staggering.

Not flowing love is not allowed in my bubble—only peace, love, prosperity, and healed wishes.
"All heals in the balloon of love, illuminating healed in God Mind."

I love it—and will use a balloon visualization rather than a bubble. A balloon is more durable and inflatable.
A healed balloon in the God Mind frequency color.

You took my thought.
A light-hearted healed balloon that makes "Ohm" sounds.

You just created an expanding universe.
Another one healing and illuminating life, yes.

I am really confident that I can manifest anything now.
All heals in God Mind, meaning you will.

And the readers of this book will heal, illuminate, and manifest their desires.
If allowing them, yes.

What would prevent them from allowing?
All doubting their healing illuminations, and God Mind flowing them.

I just thought—or you did—of a meditation people can use.

If a thought comes up that is negative, place it in a balloon of love and let it fly away.

If it is a thought of a past hurt, place it in a balloon of forgiveness and let it fly away.

Notice the beautiful blue "Ohm" balloon that has your deepest desires in it.

It gets closer and closer as it inflates and you are now inside of it, feeling only warmth, peace, and love.

The balloon expands beyond the sun, the galaxy, and nearby galaxies–with stars sparkling all around in the heavens.

You only feel Oneness in God Mind's eternal balloon, where non-love has been just a dream to be healed.

You are healed, your thoughts are healed, your wishes are healed. Nothing exists in your balloon that is unhealed.

This is your universe now.

OMG has "Ohm" in it. I love it, healing and illuminating it.

Good.
Godness illuminates goodness.

Another thought–picture the balloon being inflated from your Heart Master Portal.
Illuminating in the inflating.

Will this meditation allow readers to heal their minds and manifest their desires?
All heals illuminated in God Mind in the meditation, meaning a healed life-mind manifests its desires, so yes.

The infinite balloon is Oneness, and the stars are our DNA illuminating our wishes.
All heals illuminating in life-minds.

Face the light and all shadows will fall behind.
All illusions heal in the lightness, making no shadows.

Light has no shadows in it. Healing has no non-love in it.

God Mind illuminates in life-minds allowing only lightness.

My big, fat, OMG balloon of light is the universe of love and well-being that I am the center of.
All heals in your always projecting it now.

So be it.
Amen.

A Healing Light Machine

A friend emailed me very upset about world events. This was my reply:

"Your life is about you, and not about them. They are manifesting what they create.

The trick to life is distilling your thoughts so only the pure ones rise up.

Then you are in God Mind energy—your mind is healed, and manifests your desires.

It was never about anyone else. All they did was challenge you to reach higher.

You were facing the light with shadows falling behind you. Now you are the light where there are no shadows.

Your light is raising consciousness, and is illuminating for all who need healing. Send it to them."

A healed illumination halted non-love in her mind, allowing illumination of her healing manifestations.

I say, "There is no peace in the outer world." We can rise above life-mind thoughts to connect to God Mind, and effortlessly manifest our desires.

Lower life-mind consciousness will keep us in a state of perpetual debilitation.

Allowing healing illuminates peace—meaning your peace illuminates healed in God Mind, allowing healed manifestations into your reality.

I picture a triangle—one point is 'peace in my mind', connecting to the next point of 'healed in God Mind', then to the third point, 'manifesting in reality'.
Allowing God Mind to illuminate the triangle with love.

60-degree angles make the triangle.
A healing light machine illuminating in the life-mind, for each healing reader to remember.

Healed
in God Mind

Peace in
My Mind

Manifesting
in Reality

Don't allow life-mind non-love to ruin your beautiful, illuminated triangle.
Allow God Mind in your mind, and healing illuminates all the triangle points.

BECOMING A SAINT

Today I saw a headline about a bus accident where 6 people were killed—and many others were injured, traumatized, or just delayed.

It's hard to imagine that they all manifested their own circumstances in a group tragedy.

All healed in God Mind in their life-threatening circumstances, meaning they cleared elemental energies in halting non-love for themselves.

Life-threatening instances all heal in the life not being ended, or ending.

Because survivors are glad to be alive?

And glad healing has begun to highlight their 'accident', eliciting healing illuminations.

Did each person need the 'accident' for healing?

All allowed entering into healing circumstances.

Was the 'accident' attracted, or even orchestrated by all of them on a soul level?

'Accidents' are not accidental. Healing illuminates in all involved—meaning half in the life-mind, and half in God Mind.

All have listened to the life-mind's loss of love for itself.

Whoa. Now we're getting to the cause of the incident. Please explain.
Allowing non-love into hearts and minds halts God Mind flowing, allowing the life-mind's circumstances healing in illumination.

So the crash jolted everyone involved to love their lives, the others involved, and the ones who died and healed in death?
All healing illuminates in God Mind infinitely.

All illumination in God Mind flows into life-minds, healing in time.

Infinitely healing in time feels like time has stopped in the life-minds illuminating in timelessness.

You mentioned "non-love for themselves," and "life-mind's loss of love for itself." What are some examples of that?
Allowing halting of love means halting God Mind illumination.

Halting God Mind illumination halts illuminating life-minds allowing all thoughts of non-love.

Non-love eliminates loving illumination in all thoughts allowed to flow hate, fear, hopelessness, and injustice to others.

We have media conglomerates that try to saturate us with that—likely even on the bus.
Allowing non-love halts love.

Halting love illuminations in the life-mind allows 'accidents' to heal in them.

Healing in them eliminates more accidents, and so on.

We are not saints, and have non-loving thoughts all the time—especially if exposed to a lot of information, whether it's true or not.
Becoming a saint illuminating love is not difficult.

Heal your mind, allowing God Mind illumination.

As outlined in this book.
Illuminating and instilling the information.

Is there a difference between our spirits and our souls?
A spirit is the individual ghost of a life, meaning the illumination in time—healing in incarnating, then returning to its soul.

Are there soul groups that are all part of a larger soul?
A larger soul is incomprehensible in Oneness.

All soul groups are healed in Oneness infinitely.

How many souls are in my primary soul group?
Five souls, not including your own soul.

Did I meet them as people in my lifetime?
Not all are living now, but yes.

Are there an infinite number of soul groups?
Yes, new groups are forming into new groups, meaning half in one group form into another group, and so on.

It sounds like a school which has different grade levels, classes, clubs, etc.
All in their lifetime groups mirror their soul groups, particularly in families.

How many soul groups am I in, as an example?

Always more or less in about 15 or 16 groups.

Is it considered my soul that is in the groups, and my spirit is the aspect of my soul that accompanies the physical body in its incarnation?
Allowing alternating healing in its incarnating in its spirit in time, and in the incarnation's soul in sleep, yes.

When a child or baby dies, is it sometimes the soul's plan all along, and not necessarily anyone's fault, or a punishment, etc.?
A child cannot manifest its desires, and halts non-love routinely.

Dealing in a child's or baby's losing their life halts loving their circumstances, allowing grief to heal illuminating in God Mind.

Babies and children all heal in God Mind, allowing hope, love, and wonder in their life-minds.

Losing a child or baby has been determined and agreed upon by all in their primary soul groups.

At what age does a child start to manifest on its own?
At an age each one has non-loving thoughts.

Whoa—thoughts that will only backfire.
All thoughts illuminate or backfire on the person having them.

Backfire

(verb): to have the reverse of the desired or expected effect

That says it all.
That is all people need to know—heal in the illumination, or heal the backfire.

Where would children get most of their non-loving thoughts from?
From a media narrative eliciting hatred; from a family member eliciting hatred; and from another child eliciting hatred towards life, and him or herself. All hatred halts love and halts manifestations.

How would a child be exposed to the media narrative?
The message is embedded into all media programming, including cartoons.

All programming has a subliminal component for implanting the messages.

All elicits a feeling of powerlessness over their influences, halting loving thoughts about themselves.

If I was a parent, I would not be loving/neutral about that, actually I'd be furious.
All depending on how much television is watched, and how much guidance children are given—a lot of guidance, and a little entertainment on TV is not harmful to a healthy person.

Hatred is a cancer that starts at home—from a parent or the media—then spreads to other kids in school, etc.
All hatred halts love in the mind of the hater, making hatred the only problem.

All heals in loving the hatred healing, halting the non-love instantly in your mind.

Good point. Hating starts at home, but halting hating starts here.
All hatred halts loving, and halting loving manifests what you do not want.

Love Heals Itself

I just had a hateful thought—me hating the "hate, fear, hopelessness, and injustice to others."
Allowing them allows healing them.

How does that make sense?
All healing flows from God Mind.

Allowing healing means allowing God Mind to flow.

Flowing God Mind heals the life-mind, and so on.

But if I allow a hateful thought so it can heal, won't it manifest what I don't want—so it can heal?
All heals in flowing God Mind.

Flow God Mind the instant hateful thoughts halt loving thoughts, allowing hateful thoughts to heal.

Allowing healing illuminates in God Mind, halting incidents you do not want.

I love that!
All heals in God Mind loving itself.

Love heals itself, meaning God Mind illuminates the life-mind loving life, or God Mind.

Allow God Mind to heal the life-mind loving life.

Allowing non-loving thoughts to continue will set us back, and even be self-defeating.

A healing illumination cannot be defeated.

I want a peaceful mind, so I can manifest what I want—which is a peaceful mind, so I can manifest what I want—which is a peaceful mind, and so on—in a continuous feedback loop.
The feedback loop illuminates in God Mind, healing the life-mind to manifest in reality.

Illuminating manifestations of a peaceful mind allow healed manifestations—God-Life-Mind illuminating together.

Now that's interesting.
Now that's healing.

The more advanced you get, the fewer people you can relate to, so we'll know how you feel.
Fewer than Oneness?

Good point.
God point.

Here we go.
Everywhere we are.

You mentioned "God-Life-Mind illuminating together." How can I do that?
All healed minds illuminate in God Mind, meaning they illuminate together healed in Oneness.

Heal illuminating in Oneness by allowing love in each thought—illuminating healed in God and life-minds together—God-Life-Mind.

How will I know if I am illuminating in God-Life-Mind together?
A God-Life-Mind halts all non-love.

God-Life-Mind is love, meaning it halts all illusions from the life-mind's impermanent existence.

The life-mind's existence is a temporary illusion, healing itself into God Mind.

Very clever.
A clever hologram of light and non-light, love illuminating non-love.

"I am One with God Mind. All temporary illusions of non-love have expired today on their healing date."
Affirmations illuminate in God Mind as healed.

Goodbye, life-mind illusions.
Hello, God Mind infusion.

No more confusion.
Healed in inclusion.

All is One; illusions are done.
Healing has won.

It was allowed to win.
Allowing love in.

What happens in our life hologram if we allow only loving thoughts?

All heals illuminating in God Mind, meaning each layer of alternate illumination aligns every other level of illumination.

Aligned levels of illumination allow God Mind illumination in the life-mind, flowing healing God Mind manifestations.

Like opening a window blind all the way?

Allowing God Mind illumination to enter, yes.

You could say that each closed slat of the 'mind-blind' is a non-loving belief, thought, judgment, etc.

Allowed opening or closing in your thoughts, meaning allowing illumination in, or not.

The word 'blind' is appropriate.
Actively blinding illumination in the life-mind.

Is our life-mind hologram projected through grids or screens?
Not grids, a filament that illuminates in each layer.

How many layers are there?
Five, meaning one for each dimensionally higher filament, and including your illuminating filament.

Are layers dimensions?
All dimensions are layers, meaning all are healing in the life-mind in a layered progression, from lower to higher.

These are the 13 dimensions you had given for my last book, *Mysteries, Prophecies, and the Hollow Earth*:

Dimension 1 illuminates microorganisms

Dimension 2 illuminates minerals in the Earth

Dimension 3 illuminates most physical life in space-time

Dimension 4 illuminates life healed in timelessness

Dimension 5 illuminates no thing- meaning highly loving entities

Dimension 6 illuminates more highly enlightened intelligence

Dimension 7 illuminates in God Mind healed

Dimensions 8 through 13 all belong in the Mind of God, flowing to the other 6 unhealed dimensions.

Are the higher dimensions inside of our DNA?
All dimensions are illuminated in DNA, meaning they illuminate each dimensional layer allowed by each person's DNA.

Now I get a good picture—and suspect that they all illuminate aligned—except for our own life-mind filters.
All illuminate healed in God Mind, except the life-mind dimensional layer.

Wow.
A big exclamation elicits amazement.

It's kind of pathetic, but that's the game—heal your mind, and open the blind!
A blind healing, illuminating God Mind in each life-mind game of love, or not.

Or 'stumble around in darkness and suffer the consequences' game.
A freedom to choose game—healing in lightness, or not healing in darkness.

I think the readers all know how to win the game now, and how to heal in lightness.

All instilling explanations in this book, allowing love in their life-minds have won the game.

All can play effortlessly now.

Checkmate.

Game healed.

A Hologram Illuminates Illusions

I read that one common denominator among people who have lived over 100 years is that they had a positive attitude.

Positive thoughts heal the mind, but how do they heal the body?
A body heals only if the mind is healed.

A mental pain will cause a physical ailment, so is the body an expression of the mind?
All bodies are expressions of the filament illuminating a linear hologram from a flat surface, meaning holographic projections of a line illuminating in its own DNA.

I can see Oneness having one dimension like a dot, but what gives it 2 dimensions to be a line?
A line has a Point A and a Point B, allowing it another dimension from a one-dimensional point.

Point A is God Mind, allowing Point B as the life-mind. Illumination makes holographic illusions appearing in 3 dimensions.

What are the laws or principles governing our hologram?
All dimensions illuminate on the line, but inward— and heal illuminating outward.

I can picture the line from my mind Point B, to God Mind Point A. It heals illuminating from A to B and there are no other points?
Allowing healing illuminates in B, meaning all illumination heals in the line if allowed.

Our minds have a literal 'light switch'—On/Off, which is love/non-love.
Illuminating in the 'On' position.

It does give new meaning to Oneness if each of us is a direct line 'in' it. I was going to say 'to' it.
A linear, highly energized extension in God Mind-allowed to love in life, or not—heal in life, or not.

Always allowing love switches us 'On', and we illuminate from God Mind.
A filament healed illuminating in the Mind of God.

That manifests effortlessly.
All filaments illuminating healed in the Mind of God allow manifestations to illuminate in their line of holographic illusions.

Are my manifestations only on my A-B line?
All healing in line from B to A.

So everyone else's line of manifestation has nothing to do with me?
A holographic illusion means imaginary, so no.

I'm letting that sink in.

A hologram illuminates illusions, meaning imaginary light displays from a line, healing in line with God Mind.

A direct illuminating line to God Mind may be better imagery than a balloon.
A balloon halting non-love, illuminating your hologram is a metaphor for manifesting your life-mind desires.

A line illuminating from God Mind, healing life-mind is a metaphor for healing your life-mind illusions.

Now I'm really healed.
A healed illumination is always now—half in the life-mind, and half in God Mind—in a line.

Half in God Mind and not 'all' in God Mind?
God Mind is one-dimensional, not a line imagined in God Mind—to heal in loving life, and itself illuminating love in it.

Let's keep our line open.
Hello, can a line be open, please? I'm holding on.

Subscriber charges may occur.
All calls have half incoming, and half outgoing communication. I can compensate for half of the charges.

Don't worry, I'll manifest the other half.
Half heals illuminating in God Mind anyway.

Always now.
Always healing in the life-minds allowing illumination.

LET THERE BE LIGHT

I guess the takeaway is that we are each individual aspects of God, experiencing contrasts to know itself/ourselves—which is love.
Allowed to heal the life-mind illuminating in God Mind.

Allowed means healing—illuminating God Mind in the life-mind as loving life and itself in it.

Is the purpose of living a dream of contrasts for God Mind to know itself as the love in it?
Allowed half in the life-mind, and half in God Mind means healing is all in the life-mind, healed in God Mind.

The *Wizard of Oz* movie is a perfect metaphor for life. Dorothy died in the tornado, reunited with her soul group, and saw that her life had been a dream of contrasts.

Oneness is awakening from the dream healed.

All healing illuminated in Dorothy's dreaming her life—half in her mind, and all in God Mind.

Sometimes you say "half in God Mind."
Allowing is half in God Mind; healing is all in God Mind.

If we allow 'half and half'—in the life-mind, and in God Mind—is that referring to the left and right hemispheres of our brains?
All healing in God Mind illumination, allowed in both hemispheres of the brain, yes.

Please tell me a meditation that allows both hemispheres of the brain to heal.
A blue light illuminates the left brain, healing it loving life and itself.

Healing illumination lights in the right brain, allowing God Mind illumination in both sides.

Illuminating with the 405 nm blue color?
A light blue-magenta, filament-opening Godness frequency, meaning light, yes.

"Let there be light" illuminating in your mind.

Okay.
All heals illuminating in God Mind okay.

Okay.
Illuminating healed in God Mind is more than okay, it is perfect.

Perfect.
Okay.

Speaking of *The Wizard of Oz* movie, our conversation below is from my book, *Infinite Healing: Healed in Timelessness*.

I know many people who have died. Are they healed in timelessness?
Losing one's life means losing one's illusion in time, opening healed in timelessness.

Is it similar to when Dorothy wakes up at the ending of *The Wizard of Oz*?
In the movie, Dorothy loses her ability to imagine a world of pictures in color—healing in waking up to the monochromatic image of loving Oneness.

In the movie, color represents many flowing contrasts, allowing or not allowing love and goodness—healing or not.

Was the purpose of Dorothy's dream of life to see that she had the love, wisdom, and courage within herself?
Illuminating in time, yes.

Is that the purpose of our dream of a life?
Healing in life is healed in timelessness. Healing in losing one's life likens to a hopping toy, gaining light to hop one more time. Death illuminates life to hop again infinitely.

Is our purpose just to heal?
In life, or in losing one's life, yes.

Where was God in *The Wizard of Oz* movie?
In the love in the Tin Man, healing himself in the love for life.

In the love in the Lion, healing himself of fear.

In the love in the Scarecrow, healing himself of illogical nonsense.

And in the love of Dorothy, loving herself in all of them.

Healing in the movie motions all towards Oneness in the closing scene.

I A.M.

Is there anything I don't understand yet about how to manifest my desires?
All desires heal illuminating in God Mind as the life-mind allows them.

The life-mind allows them by loving all of life, healing itself in God Mind.

Healing itself in God Mind opens the DNA portal illumination—half in the life-mind, and half in God Mind.

Allowing DNA portal illumination heals open all in God Mind.

Loving life allows healing. Healing opens illumination halfway. Allowing the illumination heals all the way. Loving-Healing-Allowing.
Healing manifestations into life.

Loving-Healing-Allowing-Manifesting.
Healed in God Mind Allows Manifesting—I A.M.

Is that what "I A.M." means?
An acronym for 'Allowing Manifesting', yes.

You may be joking, giving me something easy to remember, but any-who...
Affirm "I allow manifesting, healing it in God Mind."

In the Loving-Healing-Allowing-Manifesting process, the Healing and Manifesting are the natural results.

We just need to do the Loving and Allowing.
"I love and I A.M." is the affirmation. "Healed in God Mind is my desire" completes it.

I am trying to identify potential obstacles to our Loving and Allowing.

Halting non-loving thoughts keeps us in Loving, or at least in neutral. What keeps us in Allowing?
A healed mind halting non-loving thoughts is Allowing.

So we only need to love life, and halt non-loving thoughts for the whole manifesting process to work?
All healed in God Mind is "I A.M. all."

I A.M. all now, so be it.
I A.M. all, amen.

In summary,

I have a neutral response to events in the world that I am not manifesting.

I have a loving response to thoughts I am healing.

I have a loving response to wishes I am manifesting.

My responses heal my mind, and allow God Mind to open in my mind.

My mind is peaceful and allows me to receive whatever I desire.
All will heal in God Mind, illuminating your affirming it.

What does God Mind respond to?
Only loving, healing, illuminating, and peaceful intentions.

Good response.
Allow it, live it, and love it.

Myself and the readers of this book will manifest worlds of goodness, as you will see.
All healed in God Mind, so I will be.

Would it be good to consider myself being in the eye of the hurricane, always in the center?
A healed metaphor, yes.

I just heard the song, 'I Can See Clearly Now' by Johnny Nash—very appropriate. I haven't heard that song in ages.

A song I sent in illumination of your 'eye of the hurricane' metaphor.

I guess that our greatest manifestation will be to reunite with pre-deceased loved ones, pets, and God Mind at the moment our lives end.
A healed illumination, yes.

Are most people surprised by this when they die?
A death means losing the unhealed life-mind—alternating healed in God Mind, and illuminating in the Light Mind.

Does the Light Mind illuminate a person's spirit?
A healed person's spirit, before reuniting with its soul.

What is a soul?
Half God Mind, and half individual healing minds activating healing illuminations in life time and placements.

Are we in constant contact with our souls?
All healed illuminations allow half God Mind, and half Light Mind instructions instilled in the life-mind.

Key word is 'healed', and what this book is about.
'Healed' means illuminating the life-mind into the Light Mind, opening in God Mind.

Not healing means life-mind illuminations lose light in fear, hopelessness, and non-loving thoughts.

That makes 'the light at the end of the tunnel' an oncoming train.
A train heading in the wrong direction, about to wreck your life-mind desires.

Then they'd really need healing.
If allowing it, meaning illuminating the wreckage that was manifested.

We've gotten off track :)
Let your track be rails of love illuminating, healing and heading into God Mind's infinite landscape.

Love illuminates the landscape, healing all passengers and crew.

All aboard!

Decouple the baggage cars.
All baggage decoupled, healing and heading out of the life-mind's dark tunnel.

An Angel of Abundance

Is there an Angel of Prosperity, or a higher being of abundance that people can call on for assistance with manifesting?
An Angel of Abundance heals all manifestations in God Mind.

What is the angel's name?
Alesi.

Will Alesi always help me to manifest my desires if I ask?
Yes.

Does Alesi have a message for me and other readers?
Alesi halts non-love in life-minds, allowing desires to illuminate healed in God Mind.

What does Alesi look like?
A light-being illuminating in the form of a woman with large wings.

Why would an angel have wings?
All healed light-beings have half human, and half flying-being characteristics—allowing them to fly, illuminate, and heal.

Super powers.
All healing in God Mind is super power.

Is there an Angel of Health?

Alesi halts life-mind non-love, healing all manifestations.

Does Alesi have a message for me and the readers of this book?

Alesi has a healing message for all who read it.

"Allow Angel Alesi to heal your mind, and advance illuminations in higher consciousness."

Achilles' Heel to Heal

I have friends, acquaintances, clients—male and female—of different religions, races, nationalities, and lifestyles than myself.

Among them are the best people I have known. We are all aspects of Oneness, represented in infinite differentiations.
Allowing you an alternate 'Achilles' Heel' to heal in appreciating them. Achilles had one weakness—his exposed heel.

Achilles healed in losing his life, allowing his heel to be hit by an arrow that had been dipped in poison.

A heel metaphor illuminates in your generous nature.

Will that be my downfall? I thought you couldn't be too generous.
A downfall occurs if you do not allow generosity a return.

Am I not allowing generosity to return?
Achilles had one flaw, allowing it to kill him. A flaw in giving is halting all receiving.

Allow generosity an Achilles' Heel to heal.

What does that have to do with diverse friendships?

Achilles had a lot of friends, and was killed by one enemy.

How can I 'heal my heel' and allow more receiving?
Affirm this, "I generously give as well as receive."

"I allow and welcome the generosity of my diverse and abundant universe."

An affirmation heals in activating its gentle generousness.

Allowing it heals Achilles' Heel.

I will also ask Alesi, the Angel of Abundance to heal any blockages that I have for receiving abundance.
Alesi heals all of them, meaning generosity flows into all of your desired manifestations.

HEALING ACTIVATION POINT

Could an affirmation heal a person's mind, allowing their body to heal from a debilitating illness such as cancer?
"All heals illuminating in my darkened closed portals—now open, illuminating in God Mind infinitely healed."

I recommend that people hold their middle fingers together, and illuminate them with 405 nm laser light—or visualize the blue-magenta light illuminating in their Heart Master Portal, while they make their wish or intention.
A filament illuminates, healing open their closed, darkened portals—meaning the life-mind heals instantly, allowing darkened portals opening to manifest physical healing in the body.

I'm a firm believer in acupressure—no pun intended. Is there a main point on the body that could be firmly pressed to allow "darkened portals opening to manifest physical healing"?
A firmly pressed healing activation point is in the middle of each person's hands and feet. Activate healing by firmly pressing in one location for 30 seconds. Healing illumination flows from Light Mind into the Light Body, allowing it to heal.

I did that for my father one night in the hospital, because he was unable to swallow—after having had a stroke the week before. The doctor said they would give it until the next day, then perform a tracheotomy surgery. The acupressure worked. My father was able to swallow soon after, and the surgery was canceled.

Healing his life-mind into God Mind allowed him to delicately swallow again.

Is the 'Light Body' our aura?
Connecting half in the Light Mind, and half in God Mind, yes.

Should I visualize, or allow my aura to be even layers of specific light colors or frequencies?
A healed aura illuminates in God Mind frequency 405 nm.

Color pictures are on the back cover of this book—the 405 nm laser light shining on a piece of quartz, and another illuminating the tetrahedron of light (made with white paper and 6-foot garden stakes).[5]

A healing, manifesting, light machine.

Readers can make a tetrahedron of light with white sheets, and easily fold it up.

A healing light machine that is inexpensive and portable.

All of the lines in a tetrahedron are equal length, and all of the angles are 60 degrees.

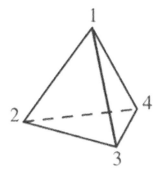

Tetrahedron

I can understand that we live in a hologram, and even that we are individually projecting it—but find it hard to understand that non-love doesn't exist because it's not in God Mind.

All non-love in holographic illusions halts God Mind flowing healing in life. Allowing it heals it, illuminating healing in God Mind.

How does allowing it heal it? Doesn't that just allow more of it?
All healing illuminates in God Mind if allowing it.

Allowing healing is fine, but not allowing non-love.
Allow healing non-love in every non-loving thought and action, healing illuminations of non-love.

It goes back to my original statement—that we project it.
All holograms are illuminations of a life-mind healing in life.

An individual's life-mind projection, or a collective projection?
An individual projection in a collective projection.

Now that's a profound thought for flowing healing.
Healing illuminates in the collective hologram projection.

Another profound thought—because I understand that in a hologram, each pixel contains the entire hologram.
Allowing each holographic illusion to heal.

There's the meaning and purpose of life—if I heal my mind of non-loving thoughts—keeping it in hope, love, wonder, peace, and gratitude—then the whole world will likewise change?
A hologram of living in a world, yes.

Life is good.
Good illuminates God.

I'll get on it.
Good.

Let's say there are people in the world who want to destroy, destabilize, depopulate—obviously not in God Mind—and may even have shit for brains... not a judgment, just an observation. Are they an illusion since they are not in God Mind?

A healing illusion allowed in holograms illuminating in each person's life-mind.

Am I personally allowing them?
Allow healing each thought of them, and each thought goes away.

Will they go away?
All heals in God Mind, illuminating in your mind, so they did go away.

Do they only exist in my mind?
Only in your non-loving thoughts.

What would I call them other than "shit for brains"?
All healing in God Mind means illuminating them in your mind heals their "shit for brains."

Do they heal, or does my universe/hologram heal?

All heals in God Mind, meaning your holographic universe.

That's good. I guess that's all that matters.
All heals in God Mind halting non-loving thoughts.

Being cynical has served me well... mostly.
All heals in being loving, not in cynicism.

Let me think about that.
All heals in deciding to illuminate loving thoughts healing the life-mind. A healed mind has decided to illuminate in loving thoughts of life, and loving thoughts of itself.

If I heal my thoughts, then I won't be adversely affected by those who are healing their 'less than healed' brains?
A healed life-mind halts non-love, so no.

Today I heard a Pink Floyd song, 'Us and Them' that stayed in my head.
Halting non-love is the meaning of the lyrics.

What would my life look like if... I mean, 'when' my thoughts are totally grateful, loving, or neutral?
A healed life-mind halting non-love allows God Mind, meaning illuminates healed in God Mind in grace.

Would I live in a state of grace?
A life-mind state of grace, allowing God Mind flowing gracefulness.

What is "grace"?
Illuminating God Mind in loving life, and allowing healing in it.

Would it significantly change my life?
Yes, healed illuminations will be effortless.

I like effortless, because I take my cues from dogs and nature—and don't exert myself unless I have to.
A healed life-mind effortlessly manifests its desires.

How long does it take to manifest effortlessly— if a person understands the principles in this book, and practices mentally every day?
About one day or more, depending on each life-mind, and each life-mind manifestation.

I thought you were going to say, "depending on God Mind's availability."
A light-hearted illumination of an absurdity, meaning healing illuminates in laughing at it.

I'm going to practice—not illuminating absurdities, but halting non-love to heal my mind, and live in GMG—God Mind Gracefulness.
"GMG, OMG, it's healing me."

Another great affirmation.
A healing illumination in life-minds.

Choose your mental home—Graceland, or a wasteland.
Healed in Graceland, or healing in a wasteland.

I choose healed.
Great choice—healed, illuminating, and allowing God Mind.

Graceful and grateful, never hateful.
Gracefully and faithfully, healing hastefully.

Graceland

A Gift to God

Is it good to detach from the life-mind, the non-love in the world—to be 'in' the world, but not 'of' the world?

It may seem heartless to not let it upset me— what happened last month, last year, or even 100 years ago.

I know there is no peace in the outer world.
A decision to heal illuminates in your mind, allowing God Mind illumination in each person's holographic universe.

Please explain.
All healing in the life-mind heals in God Mind. All healing in God Mind heals in all minds.

I'm trying to picture that.
A healed life-mind illuminates like a candle in a darkened home, meaning illuminating in one room only.

God Mind is the home, illuminating all the rooms from your candle.

Illumination heals all occupants looking for light.

Why would God Mind light up the home if one candle is lit?
A candle heals, illuminating in the life-mind.

God Mind halts non-love, allowing more healing illumination in the home.

If one mind heals, will it activate God Mind to light up the entire home—providing light for all people who are looking for it?
All allowing it, meaning all healing illumination in one life-mind illuminates healing in all minds that allow it.

That's incredible—one healed mind reaches everyone in the world?
All healing illuminates in all life-minds allowing healing, illuminating higher dimensional layers of lightness also.

It's pretty urgent for us to individually heal our minds—to be the love we want to see in the world.
A flower heals illuminating in its healing fragrance, allowing more flowers to bloom illuminating from its filament's pollen.

Be a flow-er, healing all life-minds allowing a filament highly illuminating light in their minds.

If my mind heals, does that illuminate a filament that anyone can see if they are looking?
A filament highly illuminates in all life-minds allowing healing, meaning healing illumination in your mind illuminates all life-minds allowing healing.

That is really amazing.
Healing illumination in your mind is the candle that illuminates all the rooms in the house.

So it is imperative for us to heal our life-minds to get the lights turned on—or just stay in the darkness.
A light heals, illuminating in God Mind, healing in the life-mind, and so on.

A healed life-mind halts non-love in each thought.

Should people think of themselves as partnering with God Mind to increase illumination and healing?
A partnership illuminates healed in God Mind, illuminating both partners.

A partnership requires both partners to illuminate— in the life-mind healing, and in God Mind healed.

We control the light switch, and God Mind is the light.
Healing is "On," and not healing is "Off."

Can we keep the lights on with loving thoughts, hope, wonder, and gratitude?
All heal illuminating in the life-mind, so yes.

Then I am doing the world a favor by not being drawn into the muck.
A healed favor, illuminating in your favor.

Great. We only have so many days to live—so don't spend them in the muck.
Heal, illuminate, and love all of them.

Are they a gift from God?
They are a gift to God if illuminating them.

The Only Difference

Let's review God Mind lighting up the home. A healed life-mind lights up a room, then God Mind illuminates the whole house.

Is it because more light was created by a life-mind healing?
All creation illuminates healed in God Mind, except for human life-minds.

A life-mind healing illuminates each life-mind open for healing illumination.

Each life-mind heals halting non-love, illuminating more life-minds, and so on.

No doubt that human life-minds need healing. If one mind heals, does the light that is created shine for billions of other people?
A billion or so, yes.

Would they be in 'another room of the house' and looking for the light?
A light healing illumination, yes.

Is the illumination from the new light that is created in the first healing, or does the light act as a trigger that opens portals in all DNA to receive God Mind illumination?
A healing life-mind creates light that illuminates in God Mind.

A life-mind healing illumination halts non-love, allowing God Mind loving illumination a glowing filament in the life-mind hologram.

A glowing filament halting non-love illuminates in all healing life-minds as healing intuitions.

All healing intuitions halting non-love acclimate the life-mind to more illumination, advancing in higher consciousness.

Higher consciousness accesses God Mind illumination.

Paraphrased: A healing life-mind creates light... that illuminates in God Mind... halting non-love... allowing God Mind illumination of a glowing filament in the life-mind hologram.

The glowing filament illuminates in healing life-minds as healing intuitions... that halt non-love... acclimating to more illumination... advancing in higher consciousness... and accessing God Mind illumination.
Allowed by the life-mind, or not.

If only about a billion people are open to the healing illuminations, the answer is mostly, "Not."
A crisis illuminates instead.

And most people will heal in death, and not in life.
Yes.

What would you do if you were me?
Allow delicate healing illuminations a life-mind to illuminate, alternating healing in the life-mind, and healed in God Mind.

Is the best way for me personally to do that by connecting to God Mind in nature, and not by participating in life-mind perpetual crises?
All heals in God Mind in nature, so yes.

One person healing their mind can make a huge difference.
A healing mind illumination is the only difference.

How many healed minds would it take to reach a tipping point where there are more illuminating minds than non-illuminating.
Allowing healing illumination in about 50 million people would illuminate enough filaments to heal all the rest of humanity.

That's less than 1% of the world population.
A population flowing crises to heal.

Sometimes I still get depressed by the meanness in the world—it's more than meanness—lying, killing, blaming, stealing, destroying. It's typically done by the people either with power, or with no power.
All heals in life, or in losing one's life. Healing illuminates in allowing illusions of non-love a life-mind illuminating them.

My life-mind?
All healing in one life-mind heals all life-minds allowing illumination.

Whoa.
All life-minds allowing healing illuminate in the house that God Mind illuminates.

Maybe I would cope better if I look at life as the illusion that it is—like having to watch a B-movie.
A motion picture illuminates in only 2 dimensions, allowing a life-mind to witness it from another dimension.

All flows into life in another dimension, allowing you to witness its imagery illuminating in your mind.

All non-loving imagery has one purpose—for you to heal it by allowing it.

And don't let certain scenes ruin the whole movie.
A B-movie protagonist halting non-love can be inspiration.

There are plenty to choose from.
Gandhi illuminating love is a superhero. Dr. Martin Luther King, Jr. is another hero.

I'm not looking to be that kind of hero.
A hero illuminates God Mind.

Heroism illuminates in all people that choose it.

"You must be the change you want to see in the world."
—*Mahatma Gandhi*

"Let no man pull you so low as to hate him."
—*Dr. Martin Luther King, Jr.*

ACCESSING GOD MIND

You gave me the following information in my book *Infinite Healing: Poems and Messages for the Loss of Your Animal Companion*:

What are angels?
All light beings that alternate illumination in the Light Mind and God Mind, allowing the Light Mind full healing in God Mind.

Angels illuminate the Light Minds losing light.

Is it good to call on angels in life?
A healed mind notices their lightness of being, yes.

Call on them to illuminate more of the Light Mind, healing it in God Mind.

Are pets angels?
Only healing lights in the Light Mind of pets, illuminating the life-minds of human companions.

Healing the life-mind (left brain) into the Light Mind (right brain) is the work of angels, so animal companions do the work of angels.

Not healing in the Light Mind means angels need assistance on Earth—or from nature, animals, and other people.

I would like to continue with that discussion.

Is the purpose of angels only to help us to heal, or to connect us with God Mind?

Angels will guide, illuminate, and heal the Light Mind into God Mind. All angel healing is a Light Mind illumination activated by the life-mind asking for healing.

Yes, I understand that we need to ask angels for their help, unless it is a matter of life or death where they will act independently to avert a deadly situation.
Asking angels for help will illuminate in the life-mind, healing into the Light Mind, opening in God Mind.

God Mind illuminates in eternity as healed illuminations opening in reality.

All God Mind illuminations in reality are healed illuminations that manifested what had been asked for.

Where are angels?
Angels are half illuminating in God Mind, and half illuminating in the Light Mind of Godness.

What is the "Light Mind of Godness"?
A filament illuminating in the Light Mind, opening healed in God Mind.

Is that in our minds, or are our minds connected with it?
Light Mind illuminates in the middle ring of 3 concentric rings around the Earth.[6]

---

[6] Explained in "The New Age" chapter.

Why do angels need wings to fly?
Angels fly higher in the Light Mind, accessing God Mind in the highly illuminating maneuvers.

Can angels sometimes appear in physical form?
As humans, birds, or other animals, yes—all illuminations healing the life-mind in time.

What is a good affirmation to use for requesting the help of angels?
"Angels, help me to heal my life-mind, allowing my healed mind to open in God Mind."

Would that affirmation help me to access God Mind?
Accessing it means healing in it, so yes.

What else do I need to know about angels?
Angels halt non-loving thoughts if you ask them.

Wow—that is really 'the secret'.
"Angels, heal my thoughts, illuminating my mind in God Mind" is an affirmation that will allow your desires to manifest into reality.

That could be the most powerful information so far.
Angels are more powerful than all beings, meaning angelic healing into God Mind illuminates more powerfully than healing individually.

Having angels heal my thoughts is all I really need.
A healed mind halting non-love allows God Mind, meaning 'All that is'.

And my healed mind can manifest my desires.
A healed mind allows God Mind to illuminate its desires.

God Mind illuminations manifest in reality.

I don't have many wishes other than to have a healed mind—and to manifest a life of peace, love, good health, and abundance.
A healed wish illuminates in God Mind now.

Can I do anything for you or the angels?
A healed mind illuminating lights up the house, meaning angels have more light to heal others willing to be healed. Halting non-love will be easier.

THE NEW AGE

I'm going to keep harping on this because it is the most important thing in the world.

If I raise my own consciousness to improve my well-being, it creates light that also raises mass consciousness?
All elemental filaments illuminate in life-minds allowing healing.

You had told me about mass consciousness being in 3 concentric rings around the Earth— at the day/night, dark/light line that we pass under twice a day at sunrise and sunset.

The rings are described in my book, *Sojourn*.
Concentric circles healing higher in flowing outward.

Are they part of the Earth's hologram?
A circle of healing that illuminates from the hologram's lighting in it.

You had said that the rings are:
"a low line, a middle line, and a high line in the life-mind's portal of reality...

...astounding in lighting life open in pure worlds of life loving life...

...held together with large links of life-mind love/non-love pulsing winds of neutrality...

...all in concentric circles... a line always sweeping along a light/non-light, love/ non-love, new day opening in time."

The low line is up *"about 8 miles in the upper atmosphere,"* the middle line *"about 34 miles in the stratosphere,"* and the high line *"about 144 miles in the ionosphere."*

All healing flows in an outward direction, like light illumination.

Photo credit: Kevin Gill/Flickr

What happens if I halt non-love in my mind? Does the healing create light in our hologram, activating more light from God Mind, illuminating more life-minds, and flow light outward to the rings around the Earth?

Healing flows outward, allowing holographic illumination to flow inward.

Do the concentric rings of consciousness illuminate our life-mind Earth hologram?

All will glow in healing, or darken in not healing—meaning only healing illuminates in the life-mind hologram.

Halting non-love illuminates, and non-love darkens the Earth hologram that illuminates inside the concentric rings.

A healed life-mind illuminates in the upper rings in healing itself, illuminating the Earth hologram needing healing.

Hold firmly in your conviction to heal your mind, halting non-loving thoughts.

[Humorously] What are they?
All thoughts that have healed already.

We really need as many people as possible to use their minds only for loving thoughts.
And the Earth hologram halts non-love in the New Age.

What is the "New Age"?
Illumination from the Earth hologram is so weak, that it flips the magnetic poles in about 28 more years.

Lights out, game over.
Light heals all in losing their lives, illuminating the New Age.

There's the bombshell. I refer to *The Book of Manifesting* as "the BOM."
A bomb falling illuminates in its explosion.

My last book, *Mysteries, Prophecies, and the Hollow Earth,* describes the coming pole shift and cataclysms.

Cataclysms to purify the Earth.

We're all going to die again sometime.

Healing again each time.

I'm going to heal right now, and manifest effortlessly until right then.

Filaments illuminate in the Earth's hologram to heal your illuminations.

Are we at the end of the Old Age if the New Age is starting soon?

All ages end in a geomagnetic reversal, about every 300,000 years.

Geomagnetic reversal

A geomagnetic reversal is a change in a planet's magnetic field such that the positions of magnetic north and magnetic south are interchanged. Wikipedia

What would you call the age we are in now?

An age flowing healing, allowed to heal in God Mind—or not.

'Healing in God Mind as an illusion in light' is the age name.

Activating God Mind

Is the negativity on Earth so strong that there is not enough light emitted to sustain the Earth hologram?
Not healing in illumination, yes.

What do you attribute that to?
A blinded life-mind hating life as presented in the life-mind news and entertainment. About 90% have non-loving opinions about all they are ingesting in the media.

Well, it is garbage that people are consuming.
A choice they make every day. Healing illuminates in losing power in the New Age.

Ironically, that's one bright spot—no one will miss the garbage going dark.
Allow healing illumination in life-minds now, activating God Mind, and manifesting your desires.

I imagine there is a lot of light created in people dying, but in the lower Earth rings, and not in the higher rings?
A healing illumination in the lower Earth rings will illuminate more life-minds, and not activate God Mind.

Only healing the life-mind activates God Mind—half in the outer ring, and half in God Mind.

Is that the illumination that our Earth hologram needs?
Healing illumination in God Mind halts non-love in life-minds allowing healing, so yes.

For people to heal their minds and manifest what they desire, do you recommend that they avoid negative influences?
All heal in allowing them, illuminating them in Light Mind, healing in God Mind.

I guess you can only heal it if you allow it.
A lot of people do not heal it, but hate it—not illuminating healing in their life-minds.

That's why I say to avoid it.
Avoiding illuminates in allowing, and not ingesting it.

Maybe I am cynical, but you can thank all of the haters now for extinguishing the Earth hologram.
Healing cynicism illuminates in the higher ring around the Earth, activating God Mind to illuminate the hologram.

Ok—I will heal the non-loving thoughts.
Activating God Mind, illuminating your life-mind desires.

My peaceful, loving, God Mind thoughts allow me to manifest effortlessly.

Masters have taught peace and love for ages.

God Mind has one thing to impart here.

All healed manifestations are half healed in the life-mind, and all healed in God Mind.

All healed in God Mind heals in the life-mind, allowing more healing until the halfway point.

Half illumination in the life-mind means the Earth is not fully illuminating—only half—making it not heal.

Healing the Earth means healing the mind fully.

Healing fully means God Mind delicately alternates illumination back to itself.

Alternating illumination back to itself means the healed universe disappears.

Methinks the life-mind will never fully heal.
Methinks it illuminates from you, so it is healing.

Are you saying that the sooner I heal, the sooner the universe will disappear? Or my universe anyway.
Yes.

I am healing faster than expected, so that is an alarming development in a system that runs on healing.
A healing alarm—halting non-love in an illumination alarm—like a strobe light in its notification for evacuation.

What does this mean?

Elementally, it means healing is imminent, allowing God Mind healing in the hologram.

A healed hologram has light that cannot be sustained.

Holograms allow life to illuminate, meaning illumination will cease in about 50 more years.

Is that because of the magnetic pole shift?
And Earth heals in purification.

I understand that the Earth's rotation will stop in about 50 more years because the magnetic poles flip in about 28 more years.
Allowing the Earth to reverse in rotation, and heal in purifying itself.

The end of an era.
A healing ending for humanity; a new era for Earth.

Talk about news and entertainment...
All becomes healing news in the collective life-mind, illuminating in God Mind.

How does this empower readers?
All will flow healing illumination in God Mind, illuminating in eternity.

I was trying to help them heal for practical purposes, but that sounds like a bit too much healing.
Healing in God Mind love illumination is always as much as each person needs.

Does the Earth spirit have a message before we all leave?

Earth heals in life; humans heal in life or in death.

Earth cannot heal in death, meaning it heals in renewing itself—altering the Earth's climate, lowering the temperature to purify itself.

Global freezing.

Global healing and purifying in freezing—and thawing in about 100,000 more years.

A Dream to Be Real

It's not a surprise that we're all going to die—but it's a shame that we don't know how to live.
A life-mind heals in living, healing, and illuminating in life—meaning manifesting its desires.

Illuminate all of life by loving all of it, allowing it to heal.

Death has gotten a bad rap. I explain it in my *Infinite Healing* books.
Death heals into the Light Mind, opening in God Mind. Death illuminates in loving ecstasy.

We always want to delay death, and keep on manifesting.
A death healing in Light Mind is manifesting healed illumination in Oneness.

Can we manifest "healed illumination in Oneness" while living?
Yes, allow healing of all non-loving thoughts.

You must know some tricks that Masters have used to do that.
Love halts non-love, meaning Oneness halts the illusion of twoness in the life-mind.

What is the trick to halting "the illusion of twoness in the life-mind"?

Imagining each person is yourself.

That's a brilliant idea.
Halt non-loving thoughts by meeting yourself in each person.

Cynical or not.
Cynicism heals in each one, meaning, "Not."

My relationship with each one will also heal.
A filament of healing illuminates in each one's life-mind, halting non-love toward others.

That reminds me of one candle lighting many other candles.
A candle of loving lightness.

Okay, I will do it on your recommendation.
On my illumination of each room in the house.

I'll open the blinds.
Allowing in the lightness of all creation.

One room, one house, one light.
And to all a good night.

With the light on.
Allowing the light to illuminate your dreams.

And heal my life.
A life-mind healed is a dream to be real.

That's what I feel.
Rolling like a wheel.

CREATION HAS NO LIMITS

Speaking of wheels... could you manifest for me since you are God Mind?
Allow me to, and I do manifest for you.

You could create anything I imagine, but there must be some limits.

A God Mind creation has no limits; a life-mind imagination has limits.

Let's look at an example. What if I wanted to manifest a new car—but don't need a new car, and don't want my present car wrecked or anything. I don't care if I get a new car or not, but I desire to manifest one—maybe to give it away. What would limit me from manifesting it?
A belief that new cars are not a good deal.

You got me there. How about a very slightly used car?
A car design has to be held in your imagination.

Would that give the universe 'my order'?
A car design that illuminates is God's car order—allowing it to heal in hoping, loving, and wondering about it.

Will you then set the universe in motion to fill the order?

A fulfilled healing—illuminating in God Mind is my healed order, so yes.

If I wish for peace in the world, will I only get peace in 'my world'?
All healing illuminates half in your life-mind healing, and half in God Mind healed—allowing the collective life-mind to illuminate.

The collective life-mind does heal in allowing peaceful, healed illuminations.

Can I be adversely affected by "the collective life-mind"?
Allowing it into your life-mind will manifest a collective, illuminating, healing vision that illuminates for the collective.

Allow only what you desire into loving, peaceful thoughts.

I will strive for peace in my mind.
Illuminating healed as peace in your time.

GOD MIND HAS OWNERSHIP

I would argue that present-day humans are not wired for exposure to all of the world's problems every day, since we evolved over thousands of years in nurturing and cooperative communities, most likely.
Allowing the problems heals in the life-minds owning them.

If we see them, do we own them?
Yes, how many do you want to own?

None, thank you.
Allow none into your life-mind, and none will own you.

Own me?
All that you allow to heal in the life-mind have life-mind ownership.

Is it better if I don't see them?
A healed mind detaches, and God Mind heals them.

God Mind has ownership for all that you allow to heal—meaning all healing has life-mind ownership; all healed has God Mind ownership.

For the problems in the world, all I can do is allow them to heal—and will I still own them, and they own me?
All healing in the life-mind is owned by you, and owns you.

Do I want to be healing and owning them?
A healed illusion of non-love is owned by God Mind, so heal the illusion and God Mind will own it.

How do I heal the illusion?
Acknowledge that God Mind has not healed it in your mind. Illuminating illusions will heal them.

How can I illuminate illusions?
Illuminate them healing in your mind with loving intentions.

All will heal in love in your mind, meaning God Mind has ownership.

Are they illusions because non-love does not exist in God Mind?
Yes, healed illusions are not in the life-mind, only in God Mind, and we are One.

Is there an affirmation for healing the illusions?
"God Mind heal the illusions of non-love in my mind, and hold them healed."

So, if I can't avoid seeing the world's problems, then should I have a neutral or loving response to not own them?
And them not having ownership of you.

As an example—what would it do to me if I looked at hundreds of the world's problems every day, and hated them... or hated seeing them, or hated the people causing them?

All hating halts love and limits healing, meaning healing has a lot to overcome in your life-mind.

Would my health and manifestations be adversely affected?
All of the life-mind's unhealed illusions become ailments and manifestations of what you don't want.

Whoa—I need to illuminate everything that comes up in my mind with loving intentions so God Mind owns the illusions that are now healed. My mind is healed and manifests what I desire.
A healing affirmation halting non-love.

Thank you, God Mind, for taking ownership.
All healed illusions that are allowed by you.

I must have asked this already, but what in my mind would not allow illusions to heal?
All non-loving thoughts halt healing them.

Its Appointment

Sometimes I wonder if my life is a success, because I find that it is marked by disappointment—in humanity in general, and people in particular.
All disappointment illuminates more disappointment—an appointment in 'dis', meaning allowing only love has no 'dis' integrated in it. Illuminating love disintegrates it.

The more aware I become, the more disappointing it is.
Allowing disappointment halts love, blocking manifestations that you desire.

Now that is disappointing...
All heals in allowing each disappointing thought a loving/neutral response to it.

Like what?
"A disappointing thought heals in its appointment in my loving hologram" is an affirmation to illuminate it in God Mind healed.

Can you give me an uplifting thought to replace a disappointing one?
A healed thought is one of laughter at an absurdity, such as all the world's governing bodies.

I guess they are a joke. As John Lennon said, "I want to save humanity—it's the people I can't stand."

An amusing and absurd statement.

Please tell me another absurdity.

All disappointments heal in loving them, allowing them to heal.

Yeah, I'd love them if they heal and go away.

An absurdity is loving disappointments, but it makes them go away.

John Lennon — Craig Hill Media

AN ANGEL OF LOVING TRANSACTIONS

Does money have a spirit?
An angel of all that is used in exchange, meaning all that can be ideally held in monetary exchange—not in paper money, but Gold and other commodities, yes.

What is the angel's name?
Efils.

Does Efils have a message to share?
All attachment to paper money halts in the New Age, halting in the next 28 years.

What will we need most at that time?
A source of clean drinking water, and food.

If I'm not at the source of clean water and food, what will be used to acquire them?
Acquire them before the New Age because all telecommunications and long distance travel will no longer be available in that time.

I'd have to acquire them soon using paper money.
Efils handles all acquisitions on your behalf.

Can you help me to manifest a safe, tropical home at a source of clean water and food?
A home in a delicately healing location is waiting for you and Efils to acquire it.

Can you help readers of this book to acquire what they will need?
Yes, asking Efils is always answered in the affirmative.

Do you heal our requests in God Mind so that they will manifest into reality?
Efils heals all requests in God Mind, allowing them entry into your acquisitions.

Acquisitions heal in life's transactions flowing loving intentions.

Would you be called 'The Angel of Acquisitions'?
Efils halts non-love in flowing love, meaning I am an angel of loving transactions.

Efils heals in acquiring love.

What does Efils look like?
A loving angel, half man and half light being.

Do angels wear garments?
Angels have garments like flowing robes, illuminating in white light.

Do you carry anything in your hands?
All angels carry love in their hearts and minds, allowing their hands to be free to maneuver in higher consciousness, meaning in the higher light rings around the Earth.

LOVE IS ALL THERE IS

There is God Mind and life-mind, love and non-love, infinite and temporary—you can't serve two masters.
All have halting love and allowing love, meaning there is only one master—love.

I hear ya...
Love heals all, and love illuminates God Mind—so love is all there is.

And non-love is an illusion in my mind to be healed.
A delicate illusion God Mind does not illuminate.

What illuminates it?
All non-love has illuminated in an imaginary, hopeless, alternate reality activated by fear in life-minds.

So, it's not really illuminated, just imaginary?
A healing illumination, if allowing it.

We can either allow it or love it—and allowing it is loving it because God Mind can then heal it.
God Mind illumination is love, so yes.

We can also send illumination in our minds to help heal non-love in the world.

Healing illuminations in the life-mind open into God Mind—meaning healing illuminates instantly in non-loving thoughts and actions.

As you said, "Love heals all, and love illuminates God Mind—so love is all there is." *An affirmation healing the life-mind, illuminating in God Mind, healing the life-mind, illuminating in God Mind, and so on.*

What fears in the life-mind activate the "imaginary, hopeless, alternate reality" of non-love?

- *Fear of not having enough*
- *Having enough and fearing losing it*
- *Fearing the future*
- *Fearing the imaginary perception of others*
- *Fearing having illegitimate judgments of others*
- *Fearing having the imaginary life-mind fears illuminate*
- *Fearing having the life-mind illuminations be halted*
- *Fearing having the life-mind illuminations be hated*
- *Fearing having hated illuminations be illogically halted*
- *Fearing having illogical illuminations be healed*
- *Fearing healed illuminations being illegitimate*

We've got the fears covered there.
Allow fears illumination in the truth—they do not exist in God Mind.

What does exist in God Mind?
All healing, loving thoughts of yourself and others— illuminating God Mind healing in your mind.

Is that all there is in God Mind?
"All there is" is all that is.

Does God Mind only exist in my mind?
God Mind illuminates in your mind in loving thoughts, meaning God Mind illuminates healing in your mind for you, and through you—so yes, God Mind is only in your mind—healing from the left side to the right side.

Is "All that is" only loving thoughts?
All loving thoughts and actions illuminating in the present moment, meaning healing in infinite God Mind, yes.

That gives us all the power, for sure.
All healing, illuminating in God Mind is power. All halting love is powerless.

That is very profound: "All that is" is only in our minds, in the present moment, and is the only power we have.
Allowing God Mind illumination.

Illumination of our minds?

Healing and illuminating in God Mind, flowing in life—meaning life heals, and God Mind flows.

God Mind flows more light and healing?
All flowing illuminates more healing, yes.

All from our minds?
All flows healing in the life-mind, illuminating God Mind in life, meaning yes.

God Mind is only loving thoughts, is all there is, and is only in my mind.

"All that is" is only in my mind. All that isn't is also in my mind—illusions to be healed.

The whole charade is only in my mind.
A game of charades—meaning, guess who I am now, illuminating in your mind.

You are love.
The charade is over.

GOD MIND'S GENIE

There is only one thing we can do to flow God Mind into the world—choose a loving thought in each moment, and it will let the genie out of the bottle, so to speak.
A genie that illuminates itself in the life-mind's healing in each loving thought, yes.

I'd ask the genie to heal the list of fears.
"God Mind genie, heal my imaginary fears, illuminating them healed in love" is an affirmation to God Mind's genie.

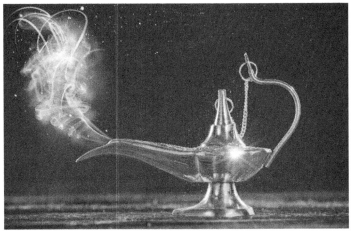

I'm a visual person. What would the God Mind genie look like?
An illumination that halts non-love in each of your thoughts, and illuminates brighter in each loving thought.

Maybe I should picture the genie on my shoulder, whispering in my ear.
A healing metaphor that illuminates in the life-mind, allowing more healing—so keep it.

Does the genie say, "Love it and allow it?"
"Allow it, love it, illuminate it, and heal it. God Mind genie halts non-love so you can heal all of it."

I like it. I mean, I love it.
All heals in loving illumination.

That's really 'All there is'.
Except for the genie, yes.

I need to heal all of the thoughts that I own, not just the problems in the world—thoughts of regret, when I could have done better; thoughts of others that are not kind, etc. When they come up, I will imagine stamping them with a big rubber stamp that says, 'I Love It'.
A blue-magenta color heals the illusions in 'The Godness Frequency'.

And God Mind will own them.
All healed illusions halting love illuminate as God Mind instruments according to God Mind.

What do you mean?
Instruments halting love, God Mind halts—making them illogical illusions in the life-mind.

Love halts the thoughts that halt love… that is illogical—because they cannot halt love if love is halting them?
All that heal are allowed to heal by you.

I'm gonna heal all of them—that's my goal anyway.
All will heal, and God Mind illuminates in eternity.

Is that because the healing creates light, and the healing is only in our minds?

Yes, illuminating God Mind infinitely.

What is the original source of the light?
A God Mind healing illusion of your life-mind in its knowing God Mind perfection—meaning halting love to know only love.

When I was really little, I asked my mother, "Who made God?" after asking who made the world, etc.
All that heals creates God, meaning all that is healed is God—illuminating in your mind to heal, and so on.

That's not the answer I got, but did the healing come first to create the healed God?
All healing is only in your mind, meaning 'All that is' comes from you.

I'll think about that—but in the meantime, manifesting will be easy if 'All that is' comes from me.
A healed God Mind illumination flows into all of your manifestations.

I love it.
Heal it, allow it, flow it, love it.

THE LIFE-MIND/GOD MIND CONNECTION

Are there 10 Commandments? I think there are only 2 that cover them all: "Love God with all your heart and mind," and "Love your neighbor as (well as) yourself." They are more like strong recommendations than Commandments.

"Allow God Mind healing into life by loving all of it, allowing it healing in God Mind" is the life-mind/God Mind connection to all that is—meaning all illumination in God Mind.

What would you call it?

A flowing, healing illumination for commanding God Mind healing, illumination, and flowing.

Choose it, and use it.

Allow God Mind to infuse it.

No way to confuse it, or abuse it.

Healing illuminates in who's it. Excuse it, meaning my grammar.

I can use it.

Heal it, and don't lose it or snooze it. Allow healing to defuse all twoness, and I'll include it.

GENEROSITY COMES BACK

The best investment may be giving money away, because it comes right back with interest. This week, I decided to always give $1 bills to those asking on street corners, and did so. I then sent money to a man with 15 dogs in a war-torn country. The next day, I found a crisp $100 bill on the floor of my car—and the car had been thoroughly cleaned the previous week.

A bill is a bill. Increments don't illuminate, only the bills—meaning healing halts selfishness, allowing bills to appear in your life.

Did the bill just appear, or had I dropped it at another time?

A bill appeared half illuminating in time, and half illuminating in timelessness as your generosity.

Generosity comes back, illuminating in time.

With interest.

Always illuminating more in multiples of the generosity illuminated in the original giving.

I thought the $100 bill must have appeared, because I don't typically carry $100 bills... or drop them... and not notice.

A bill has illumination abilities—allowing healing illuminates them; halting healing halts illuminating them.

Can money magically come and go?

A healed mind illuminates the money it desires; a healing mind halts money in its non-loving thoughts and actions.

You said, "A bill has illumination abilities." Please explain.

A healed illumination means it illuminates in timelessness. Money exists illuminating in timelessness also.

Heal money illuminations by giving it generously, and it will illuminate healed in your life generously.

That makes a lot of sense... or cents :)

All healing in the life-mind is illogical; all healing in God Mind makes sense.

Why is healing in the life-mind illogical?

Because the life-mind halts love and looks for love at the same time.

Our job is to heal the life-mind and see only love.

Allow only love, and love halts non-love in your life— illuminating your desires.

MORE GOD THAN MONEY

Is money energy as people sometimes say?
All has energy in God Mind electrons, allowing God Mind to heal in illumination.

Do you mean physical money? What about really large amounts that are not physical cash?
All have God Mind electrons in imagining them.

If I only imagine a large amount of money, does it have God Mind electrons?
A healed imagining has God Mind electrons; non-healed imaginings do not have them.

That's very interesting in several respects— mainly that healed imaginings become real.
All healed imaginings have God Mind electrons— halting non-love, allowing love into life-minds.

Love is real, and everything else is an illusion— or love is light, and everything else is a shadow.
God Mind illuminates love—all else is not in God Mind, or it would illuminate in love.

What would be a "healed imagining" of money?
A generous, healing, loving, and beautiful imagining.

Could you please give me an example?
An imagined, healing, beautiful, generous, loving thought of money would be holding it in your heart

and mind—half *illuminating* in *God Mind* in *timelessness, and half illuminating in God Mind in time—all healing in the life-mind in the present moment.*

All healed in the present moment illuminates God Mind in eternity.

Should I picture the money healing?
Illuminating healed, yes.

Is there unhealed money?
Greed is fear and halts love, meaning it is unhealed.

I'm thinking that money is neutral—but if I imagine it healed, does that mean it heals only for me?
All healing is only for you, so yes.

Do I need to have healing thoughts about the money, or how to use it—or just illuminate it in my mind?
Illuminating it heals it—meaning it halts non-love in its illumination, allowing God Mind to illuminate in it—healing all it is in contact with.

So, if I illuminate it in my mind, it becomes healing money.
Your healing money, yes.

Healed money.
Healed in your imagining; healing in the life-mind's illuminating it healed.

Is the money healed in timelessness, and healing in time?
Yes, illuminating it healed in eternity.

Can I heal all money? Maybe then it will all be used for healing purposes.
All God Mind electrons heal, illuminating in eternity, so yes.

What would it be called then?
God's healed money.

I guess we won't be able to say "more money than God" anymore :)
Laughing heals, illuminating in God Mind.

God Mind illuminating healed in all the money in the world would be more God than money, but healing illuminations in the money would be more healing than money could buy.

HEALING THE LIFE-MIND IS ENOUGH

Do I have any beliefs that are limiting my manifesting ability?
A belief halting manifestations, achievements, and is debilitating illuminates half in fear, and half in beliefs.

Facing it heals it—illuminating half in the life-mind, and all in God Mind.

What is the belief?
A belief in having enough in life halts having enough in life.

What do you mean?
"Having enough" in life means illuminations in life are not enough. Affirm that healing the life-mind is enough.

Healing my life-mind is enough. It is all I will ever need, allowing me to have no needs.
Healing illuminates in the life-mind, opening in God Mind as no needs.

I believe that my mind is healed and needs nothing.
I believe healing halts limits, illuminating manifestations.

I have enough because my mind is healed.
A healed mind manifests its desires.

I am like God Mind and don't need anything.
A healing affirmation illuminating the life-mind, allowing all desires to effortlessly manifest.

My desire is only for a healed mind.
A God Mind illumination in the life-mind allows more God Mind illumination in Life-God-Mind, and so on.

Does a Life-God-Mind see only love and Oneness?
All God Mind illumination in the life-mind is loving Oneness, so illuminating Life-God-Mind illuminates God Mind in life, meaning illuminates in yourself.

Making us One.
One love in one life-mind, illuminating one God Mind, yes.

ALLOWING US TO BE ONE

Could we have DNA portals that are closed because of our ancestors—their beliefs, or lack of abundance, etc.?
All portals are opened in your allowing healed, loving thoughts because they flow through them.

Now that's interesting!
Healed, loving thoughts flow illuminating in healed manifestations.

All healed illuminations manifest in physical reality.

It's really that simple, or should be...heal your thoughts to be only loving; then manifest your desires. If you can manifest your desires, why would you have a non-loving thought?
A belief illuminates in its healed open portal, or closes an unhealed portal.

Are you saying that we could have unhealed beliefs that we are not aware of, and they would be limiting our abundance?
All heal in affirming this: "All my beliefs heal illuminating in lovingness and kindness, allowing Oneness to be my belief."

Wow—that's powerful. I just felt a quadrillion portals open :)

About a billion flow illuminations of abundance into your life.

I believe you—I mean, I believe in allowing Oneness.
A belief illuminates healed in God Mind, flowing healed in the life-mind, allowing us to be One.

Are any religious beliefs useful?
Only a belief in flowing God Mind loving into life to heal itself is believable.

The poem "I Believe" from my book *The Lightness of Being* comes to mind— conversations with Oneness written in rhyming verse.

I BELIEVE

> I don't believe
>   I'm just sayin'
> but I'd like to relieve
>   some thoughts I've been prayin'
>
> to some degree
>   nothing is free
> and if I have to believe
>   I will believe in me
>
> *I don't believe either*
>   *so I'm with you*
> *since there's only love*
>   *only love will do*

you prayed for strength
  and I gave you courage
to hold onto your vision
  and not be discouraged

you prayed for truth
  and got spiritual eyes
to see to the root
  behind all the lies

I'm just sayin'
  the answer is 'yes'
to what you've been prayin'
  and to your requests

the only thing
  you had asked of me
was for strength and truth
  you were ready to receive

it was always there
  inside of your heart
where you can truly feel
  we are not apart

talk about truth
  and the courage to see
that you're One with me
  then I believe we agree

Flowing Freedom Money

I'm not so much interested in the money as in the freedom it will allow. Besides a flow of income and good health, what else would I need?
A healed mind.

Because a healed mind can manifest abundance and good health?
All depending on how much healing illuminates.

How could I have maximum healing illumination?
A healed illumination halts all non-loving thoughts, illuminating healing in all loving thoughts.

Should I focus on loving the freedom and well-being?
A flowing healing, illuminating God Mind, all accepting, halting illogical non-love, illumination in the life-mind, yes.

What could I visualize to capture that feeling?
Picture a large, heated, illuminating, and flowing pool of water that halts non-love in the life-mind.

The pool of illuminating water is God Mind loving goodness, allowing you to float in absolute peace.

God Mind's pool of water halts non-love, meaning healing illuminates only in its flowing love.

And stay in the water.
All healing illuminates in the water—meaning as God Mind, the healing pool is "all there is."

Do loving thoughts make me one with the water, since the water is only loving thoughts?
Yes, illuminating in eternity as God Mind, healing in the life-mind in time and placement.

Nothing really exists outside of the God Mind flowing pool, except non-pool illusions that need to heal into the pool.
All illuminating in the life-mind heals into the God Mind flowing pool.

That is important because it seems like I am responsible for what heals into the pool.
All healed illuminations increase the infinite pool, illogically.

Does that make me personally responsible for illuminating the universe hologram, and perpetuating infinity?
Enlightening the life-mind illuminates God Mind, meaning healing the life-mind allows God Mind illumination, so yes.

My pool is expanding because of all the money :)
Flowing freedom money illuminates in life, and manifests for you now.

I'm stayin' in the pool.
All flows healed in it—so am I.

I can't believe it—well, yes I can believe it—but I just found another crisp new $100 bill in my car! Now I know it's definitely not from me because the one I found there last week is still in my pocket, and I'm the only one who uses the car.

A bill flowing enough halted not having enough.

All I want is a healed mind.

A bill halts not having enough from a healed mind.

Lemme go check my lottery ticket :)

A healed mind illuminating a lottery win allows a lottery winner.

I don't care, so I'll check it next week. If, I mean *when* the win comes, I will give a lot of the money away.

All heals illuminating in generosity.

When we express love it creates light, perpetuates infinity, and the universe expands. Does that illogically create more than "all there is"?

"All there is" halting non-love, healing and illuminating in God Mind increases "all there is", meaning illumination in God Mind allowed by healing in life-minds halting non-love increases in God Mind.

So, I guess "all there is" could expand or contract and still be "all there is."
More healing illumination is more than what is; God Mind love in life is "all there is."

More magical $100 bills are more than what was :)
All that heals is more than what was.

My healed mind is what will be—and my unhealed mind will be what was.
Illuminating "all there is."

Another poem from *The Lightness of Being:*

MORE THAN WHAT IS

What I need
   is goodness and peace
so how can I find
   both of these

I've seen examples
   of what they can be
but no longer believe
   that they come only from me

maybe they do
   or don't even exist
at least not in abundance
   and there is no bliss

Now there's a puzzle
   and you have something to do
to find more pieces
   that bring peace to you

I like dogs
flowers and poems
to see the birds
and to be at home

quite a bore
I already know
but I like to explore
the realm of unknown

let's cut to the chase
tell me some more
what is reality
what is it for?

I'm tired of anger
bitterness and hate
don't tell me about fear
or what I create

not while I'm here
marooned out in space
with villains and goons
always in my face

at least in the news
what a disgrace
humanity is doomed
and picking up the pace

That's their world view
they have film crews to make
enough to confuse
the whole human race

it's not about them
it's only about you
and the way that you feel
in each moment that's new

do you feel excited
to have one more chance
another day in your life
to see your soul advance?

remember again
what you like to see
the love of dogs
and birds and flowers being free

see what they teach
and what you said you need
exploring love and peace
and how you reached me

expanding my Oneness
beyond All That Is
like poems out of nothing
is why creation exists

All becomes more
you're inflating What Is
not at all a bore
you're making great bliss

here's a contradiction
the news won't report
if there's All That Is
how could there be more?

the universe expands
in only one direction
and when I say in
I mean introspection

look inside
as you've been meaning to do
and when I say meaning
means it's meant for you

so you are the receiver
    creating goodness that lives
with peace in each moment
    you're now More Than What Is

(and another clue
    that you can use
is that your goodness and peace
    others could use too)

In my book, *Poems of Life, Love, and the Meaning of Meaning*, I asked you what the universe expands into, and you said, "Right into you... farther than self-love can peacefully go."
How can it expand in any other direction on a line that is infinite in one direction?

Is inward infinite?
All healed in God Mind is infinite, meaning your God Mind higher self illuminates infinitely.

In one direction.
Inward illumination in God Mind is outward illumination in life.

Hmm...
Allowing the life-mind to illuminate healed in the Light Mind, opening in God Mind—in a circular feedback loop, flowing eternally.

MORE THAN ANYONE CAN AFFORD

What is 'structured water'?
All water healed in its God Mind electrons halting non-love, and halting non-beneficial energies.

Because of its atomic structure?
All atoms halt non-love or allow non-love, depending on illumination from life-minds.

Meaning that it is our intentions that use them for love or non-love?
All loving intentions heal atomic structures; all non-loving intentions malign them.

Is that how intentions can heal?
All healing illuminates intentions, so yes.

Is 'structured water' miracle water?
All water has half God Mind, and half life-mind properties flowing healing illumination in life.

Allow half in God Mind to illuminate half in life-minds.

How can I do that?
Allow half illuminating in God Mind to willingly halt non-love in the life-mind by asking before drinking or bathing.

Allow it to heal, illuminating your life-mind in loving life.

Should it be cleared of negative information first?
Halting non-love in the life-mind is clearing all that is negative.

By asking?
Asking, allowing, and actively illuminating it.

Can we make it healing water by adding our intentions?
Allowing God Mind healing in the flowing it, yes.

On another occasion we had discussed making structured water by running it through a 14-inch piece of 2-inch diameter bamboo, filled with river stones.
A halting non-love, healing filter from nature.

Does structured water have non-love removed from it?
God Mind heals illuminating in it, yes.

Do impurities or non-loving thought forms in regular tap water halt God Mind from illuminating in it?
Allowing the non-love half into life, yes.

To purify the water, is it best to ask, or to run it through the stone filter—or both?
A filter eliminates the 5 main energies adversely affecting humanity. #1 Avarice, #2 Greed, #3 Hatred. #4 Envy, #5 Decadence.

A lot of nasty stuff. We need industrial scale stone filters everywhere—and unfortunately we are also made mostly of water.
A filter in each home is enough to halt non-love in humanity.

Wow, and it wouldn't really even cost anything either.
Avarice, greed, hatred, envy, and decadence all cost more than anyone can afford.

I'm going to find a source for bamboo, and remove non-love from the water I drink. Would it become miracle water because God Mind in it is now allowed to flow?
A God Mind healing, flowing, illuminating, actively God Mind instilling—fountain of love.

If I focused my healing intentions into the water and drank it, would they manifest in reality?
All heals in God Mind flowing in it, so yes.

For the birds and plants outside on a larger scale, would 'flowforms' work just as well?
A flowform halts non-love in life, so yes.

Flowform.
Photo credit: carljosephpaola.com

HEALING FINANCIAL AND MONETARY LOSSES

We had once discussed shining a red light on 3 of the left-hand fingers to manifest money.
Altering the healing portals into opening, healing financial and monetary losses.

How do I do that?
Illuminate 3 left fingers—thumb, middle finger, and ring finger—with a light in the longer wavelengths of red and orange.

Ask for healing in financial and money matters, allowing the healing portals to illuminate.

Healing portals illuminate open in the Mind of God.

For how long should I illuminate those fingers?
About 5 minutes.

What is a "healing portal"?
A healing portal in DNA that illuminates in God Mind, allowing healing illumination in the life-mind.

Healing portals include all of the half life-mind, and half God Mind illumination in the life-mind's healing projection.

Healing illuminates half in the life-mind, and all in God Mind.

Then would all DNA portals be healing portals?

All healing portals are in DNA, but not all illuminate in the life-mind.

Healing requires the life-mind to illuminate.

Will some portals always be in the dark?
A darkened, closed healing portal will not open in the life-mind in the current lifetime.

Why not?
A closed portal heals open in its lifetime agreements allowed to illuminate.

Please give me an example of a closed portal that was agreed to not be allowed to heal open in this lifetime.
Agreeing to heal in the host body illuminating is one example.

When we die, do all of our DNA portals heal open?
All heal open in the Mind of God, yes.

Have some people agreed to be poor in this lifetime, with closed money portals that cannot heal?
A healed life-mind heals them all open.

It makes sense that they can heal—since we are here to heal—but you said some will not open.
All financial and healing portals will open if illuminating in the life-mind.

How many DNA portals are there?
Almost 5.5 quadrillion.

Why so many?
Allowing the life-mind infinite flowing possibilities illuminating in life, to heal in God Mind.

What percentage are we able to heal open?
About 84%.

How big are the DNA portals?
Illuminated open, they are half the size of a light photon on one side, and infinite on the other side.

Halting non-love opens them infinitely on both sides.

What are some of the things we could do or manifest by opening our DNA portals?
Anything that God Mind can flow into the life-mind.

Like what?
Any healing illumination that you imagine.

Do we open our DNA portals with loving intentions?
All feelings either open or close the portals.

Do neutral to joyful feelings open our DNA portals?
All feelings of hope, love, and wonder illuminate them open.

Do wild animals close portals to God Mind with their thoughts or feelings?
All animals can close or open any God Mind portal in their DNA.

Can animals open some portals that humans cannot?
All humans are half animals, so they can heal and illuminate their portals open to God Mind.

If humans are half animals, what is the other half?
A light being that has incarnated, illuminating in a light activating body.

For what purpose?
To heal in time and motion in place—allowing God Mind illumination a Light Mind alternating in the life-mind, actively manifesting its desires.

Why?
God Mind heals illuminating in life, creating more light, perpetuating infinity.

Another poem from my book *The Lightness of Being* comes to mind.

WHAT WILL SURELY BE

The tiniest atoms
　　that we cannot see
how could it be
　　that they would agree

to form into elements
  one hundred and eighteen
making molecules and cells
  then into organs and me

forming animals and plants
  the earth and seas
the entire cosmos
  to infinite degrees

Let's back up
  to where you said 'me'
to find love in the order
  and what do you see?

there's only one place
  where balance breaks down
but it forms your reality
  and it's only found

in your thoughts
  and in your beliefs
in fear and doubts
  or in love and peace

what powers your atoms
  each creative and free
the love of Godness
  your power is me

(and in this moment
  when we always meet
is where atoms create
  what will surely be)

THE HIGHLIGHT FREQUENCY

Can we manifest our desires by shining other light wavelengths on our fingers?

We have discussed the shorter blue ultraviolet, and the longer red wavelengths.
Eight fingers heal by flowing light outward into life's activities in place and time.

All heals in this frequency of invisible light called 'the highlight frequency'.

Highlight frequencies on one hand illuminate fingers on the other hand when hands are held together.

Hold hands firmly together to illuminate healing intentions in your life-mind.

Intentions heal, illuminating in open portals—half in the life-mind, and all in God Mind.

Healed intentions manifest in physical reality.

Would you call that 'praying'?
All healing intentions are prayers—illuminating healing in the life-mind, and healed illuminated in God Mind.

Illuminations healed in God Mind are life-mind manifestations.

Is the answer to peaceful, healing prayer requests always "Yes"?

Always, if allowing an affirmative answer.

So if the answer is not affirmative, is that what the person unconsciously wants?
All responses are affirmative. Not allowing halts an affirmative healing response.

Often a person prays for their family, or another person.
All flows healing illumination in another life-mind, actively manifesting healing in them.

Should we pray for guidance, healing, patience, and understanding?
And allowing delicate successes to illuminate all day and all night long.

Please tell me a good prayer to use.
"God, heal my intentions for illuminating my life-mind, allowing my intentions to manifest, illuminating all who heal from them."

That's really great. I would also ask angels to help heal the intentions, and illuminate my life-mind.

Angels illuminate all healing intentions, halting non-love and not allowing.

That's awesome.

All angels are awe-inspiring, healed illuminations in God Mind, illuminating in life-minds requesting their illumination.

What is a good request to ask an angel?

"Angel, please heal my intention of halting non-love in my mind, connecting my mind to God Mind, allowing my manifestations.

Halting non-love in my mind allows only love in my life, and illuminates my manifestations."

In my book *Infinite Healing, Healed in Timelessness*, you said that we are each assigned a loving guardian angel at birth.

All people have an angel, animals have nature spirits, all plants have internal spirits, all minerals have mineral spirits, and all micro-organisms have an upper and lower spirit, depending on the lifetime function of the organism.

And the angel will help us throughout our lives as long as we ask, and then listen?

Listen, and then heed the angel's guidance.

THE LIGHT THAT IS CREATED

What is the most powerful manifesting technique in this book?
A holding open of illuminations healed in each loving thought.

If I hug my pet and say, "I love you," is that God?
All God is loving, healed thoughts, so yes.

God is the thought, correct?
God is the healed thought, meaning it is the light that is created in the healed illumination of thought.

Is God the light that we illuminate, and it illuminates us through our DNA portals that are open?
A light halting non-love illuminating in a holographic illusion allowed by the life-mind, yes.

I love you, God.
God is love allowed in your life-mind, meaning I am illuminating healing in you.

God illuminates as you loving life and myself.

GOD NIGHT

I keep trying to conclude this conversation, but don't really want to. "Keep trying" is not the right affirmation, but do you have any other advanced spiritual concepts to share with all of us healed minds?
Knock, knock.

Who's there?
Al.

Al who?
Al heals in me, illuminating in you.

I need to heal from that joke.
Al-low it.

Al-ways.
Al-right.

And to Al a good night.
God night.

God night, Al. Now we're on the same page.
Healing Al night and Al day, God Mind flows love, Al the way.

Al is perfect in my world.
Amen. Al will be.

Readers should be good to go then—if they keep in mind the principles of this book.
'Good' means 'God', so they are 'God to go'— Illuminating illusions, eliminating confusion, love's inclusion is God Mind's infusion.

Okay, I can see where this is going.
Healing and flowing, illumination glowing.

The readers are growing.
In their God Mind knowing.

God night.
God light.

Readers can continue this dialogue with you. I am trying to reach an uplifting conclusion.
All heals illuminating in God Mind, meaning all readers who halt non-love allow God Mind into their minds.

The End.
Healing illuminations never end.

And now is when.
Allowing intends, healing mends.

You and the readers are friends.
Healing depends on what the life-mind sends.

Love heals... sending now.
God Mind feels, illumination is how.

I'm glad you have a healing answer for everything, and everyone.
God Mind healing illuminates life as One.

Love is One, everything else is an illusion.
Illusion's healing begun, non-love is done.

I'll leave it there.
Healing everywhere.

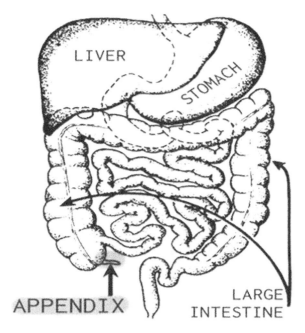

Photo credit: realfarmacy.com

Very funny. Was that your idea?
Yes.

You were probably feeding me lines in high school. I could have gotten into a lot of trouble.
All the good ones, meaning they allowed you to stay out of trouble—healing life-minds illuminating in laughter.

One last question—where are you, meaning where is God?
Where healing, loving, and peaceful thoughts are—having no other place to live.

AFTERWORD

Now I'm thinking that if our lives are dreams that seem real, then is the spirit world real and it seems like a dream?
All in the spirit world is a real attempt at God Mind illuminating in twoness.

Could God Mind attempt something and not be successful?
A God Mind attempt is all in life-minds attempting to be real illuminations of love.

Either a poor attempt or a hugely successful attempt.
A failed attempt is still an attempt.

So, if I was fully in the spirit world and no longer had a body, would it seem real to me?
Alternating between healing and healed—meaning it alternates healed in God Mind as real, and in the Light Mind as a healing illusion.

What is it like to be in the real God Mind?
God Mind is all lovingness, acceptance, gentleness, and holistic God Mind Oneness acclimating your mind to the thought of God Mind being yourself.

Can you please outline exercises or practices that readers can do regularly to heal their minds?

Currently, I visualize myself for 1 minute in a Merkabah that is illuminating blue-magenta.
Do 4 exercises every morning, and every night before going to sleep.

The same 4 exercises?
Yes.

Exercise 1: Hold index fingers together, and flow only loving intentions to God Mind for 1 minute.

Exercise 2: Hold all fingers together, hands facing each other. Ask God Mind to halt non-love in your thoughts for 1 minute.

Exercise 3: Hold 4 fingers in opposite correlations together, and love allowing non-love in a life-mind's illogical illusion for 1 minute or more.

Exercise 4: Invite healing into the life-mind for 1 minute or more.

What will that do?
The life-mind heals, illuminates, and flows God Mind.

[Humorously] God Mind will flow for more than 1 minute, correct?
God Mind flows, heals, and illuminates a life-mind entering into God Mind for as long as the life-mind allows it with loving thoughts.

I have an exercise for God Mind—4 times in the morning, and 4 times in the evening. Heal the minds of myself and the readers of this book for 1 minute or more. It will help God Mind to flow freely.
A healing exercise I do in no time, meaning in timelessness—allowed into time only by you.

We can exercise together.
As One? I like it!

Don't you love it?
Allowing it is loving it.

Yeah, we went over that in Chapter 6.
Good.

Good is God.
Okay.

Okay, good.
God is perfection.

Okay, perfect.
Good.

AFFIRMATIONS

"Love your life now, and the future will be what you desire." (pg. 37)

"All heals in my mind, manifesting in my life in the perfect time." (pg. 38)

"Allowing God Mind goodness is my hope, love, and wonder in life." (pg. 45)

"I am illuminating healed, allowing love in my life" (or money, health, peace, or prosperity). (pg. 56)

"All flows into my life in love." (pg. 57)

"I am illuminating healed, allowing money into my life. I illuminate it in my hands and in loving life's goodness." (pg. 57)

"All will heal in my life in God Mind, and in my mind. Healing in my mind allows my desires to manifest.

All heals in my mind and in God Mind willingly and lovingly by including more than $30,000.

Allowing $30,000 into my life lowers my obligations and my needs, healing all of them.

I love my money healing my mind, illuminating in God Mind—manifesting in my life, allowing my life to heal." (pg. 56)

"I welcome money to flow through my life like a river, healing wherever it goes, illuminating life wherever it heals." (pg. 57)

"Allow him his inconsiderations healing in God Mind. God Mind heals my mind, allowing only peacefulness." (pg. 64)

"This is my healed illumination. I love it, allow it, and live it." (pg. 67)

"All heals in my mind, illuminating in God Mind, manifesting my peaceful desires." (pg. 70)

"Flowing healing light illuminating from God Mind heals my universe flowing from my mind." (pg. 77)

"Everything is perfect in my world." (pg. 89)

"All heals illuminating in God Mind, allowing illumination of my manifestation." (pg. 116)

"I am healed in God Mind since losing my illusions, allowing illumination of my manifestation" (pg. 131)

"All heals in my mind; all is healed in God Mind. I love all of life healing me." (pg. 137)

"All heals in the balloon of love, illuminating healed in God Mind." (pg. 144)

"I am One with God Mind. All temporary illusions of non-love have expired today on their healing date." (pg. 158)

"I allow manifesting, healing it in God Mind." (pg. 171)

"I love and I A.M. Healed in God Mind is my desire." (pg. 172)

"Allow Angel Alesi to heal your mind, and advance illuminations in higher consciousness." (pg. 178)

"I generously give as well as receive. I allow and welcome the generosity of my diverse and abundant universe." (pg. 180)

"All heals illuminating in my darkened closed portals—now open, illuminating in God Mind infinitely healed." (pg. 181)

"GMG, OMG, it's healing me." (pg. 189)

"Angels, help me to heal my life-mind, allowing my healed mind to open in God Mind." (pg. 201)

"Angels, heal my thoughts, illuminating my mind in God Mind." (pg. 201)

"God Mind heal the illusions of non-love in my mind, and hold them healed." (pg. 217)

"My mind is healed and manifests what I desire." (pg. 218)

"A disappointing thought heals in its appointment in my loving hologram." (pg. 219)

"Love heals all, and love illuminates God Mind—so love is all there is." (pg. 227)

"God Mind genie, heal my imaginary fears, illuminating them healed in love." (pg. 227)

"Allow it, love it, illuminate it, and heal it. God Mind genie halts non-love so you can heal all of it." (pg. 228)

"Allow God Mind healing into life by loving all of it, allowing it healing in God Mind." (pg. 231)

"Healing my life-mind is enough. It is all I will ever need, allowing me to have no needs." (pg. 238)

"I believe that my mind is healed and needs nothing." (pg. 238)

"All my beliefs heal illuminating in lovingness and kindness, allowing Oneness to be my belief." (pg. 240)

"God, heal my intentions for illuminating my life-mind, allowing my intentions to manifest, illuminating all who heal from them." (pg. 261)

"Angel, please heal my intention of halting non-love in my mind, connecting my mind to God Mind, allowing my manifestations.

Halting non-love in my mind allows only love in my life, and illuminates my manifestations." (pg. 262)

GLOSSARY

Oneness: Infinity healed illuminating in God Mind.

God Mind: All twoness healed and illuminating in Oneness.

Life-mind: Left-brain hemispheres healing and illuminating in an open portal in time.

Light Mind: Right-brain hemispheres opening into the Mind of God.

Light Mind of Godness: Alternating healing and healed in life-mind allowing God Mind.

Portal: An opening in DNA, lighting open in God Mind.

Filaments: Undulating light sensors, halting or allowing light into life through life's DNA.

Illumination: A healing light in your mind, or a healed light in God Mind.

Light: All electrons and photons flowing into life.

Timelessness: All healed in God Mind, not in the life-mind.

Time: The lightness of being alternating in the life-mind as the illusion of moving in a progression.

Nature: All of life healing in the Mind of God.

Death: Lighting open healed infinitely in Oneness.

Infinity: All one instant in the Mind of God.

"For good alone may wholly, materially manifest in an earthly world."

—*Edgar Cayce*

FURTHER READING

For more on soul groups and the soul's experience, I recommend the books by Michael Newton, Ph.D.

Journey of Souls

Destiny of Souls

I also recommend the following God Mind books channeled by the late Jean K. Foster (godmindbooks. wordpress.com).

The God-Mind Connection

The Truth That Goes Unclaimed

Eternal Gold

Decision

New Earth, New Truth

Masters of Greatness

Divine Partnership

Epilogue

From *The Lightness of Being:*

I GOOGLED GOD

I googled God
   and they had his picture
did I say 'His'
   the same as in scripture

kind of old
   up in a cloud
lack of oxygen
   created a shroud

Quite a mystery
   my appearance
always here
   in a sheer coherence

being the opposite
   of whatever you fear
and forever near
   with no interference

I like to hear
   of your adherence
only to love
   and of fear's disappearance

that's what I look like
   or how I appear to you
and you'll look like me
   when you are love too

so to google God
   just look in a mirror
I am still clear
   and you will see me clearer

ABOUT THE AUTHOR

From God Mind:

Paul Gorman illuminates as a spiritual researcher,
writing his discoveries into books,
allowing healing in the minds
of all who read them.

Made in the USA
Las Vegas, NV
04 January 2025

15727623R00173